SpringerBriefs in Law

For further volumes:
http://www.springer.com/series/10164

Fábio P. Shecaira

Legal Scholarship
as a Source of Law

🐎 Springer

Fábio P. Shecaira
Federal University of Rio de Janeiro
Rio de Janeiro
Brazil

ISSN 2192-855X   ISSN 2192-8568   (electronic)
ISBN 978-3-319-00427-3   ISBN 978-3-319-00428-0   (eBook)
DOI 10.1007/978-3-319-00428-0
Springer Cham Heidelberg New York Dordrecht London

Library of Congress Control Number: 2013939345

Printed on acid-free paper

Springer is part of Springer Science+Business Media (www.springer.com)

Where does the court find its law? Where does any one find law? That part which is not found in the judge's breast, in the kind of person he is, in his sense of justice, in his education and his environment, must be found in books. What books? We have been taught to answer: the books containing the statutes and the reported decisions: And it is still a correct answer, as far as it goes. But—I think we shall have to admit—it does not go as far in 1928 as it did in 1828. Courts rely for guidance not merely on their understanding of the statutes, not merely on precedents in their own and other jurisdictions, but also on books, on treatises written by persons whose only authority was the learning they displayed.

Max Radin, Sources of Law—New and Old

In other words, one may pay attention to theses developed in legal writing not only because of the quality of the reasons proffered therein, but also due to the authoritative position that legal writers occupy. It is a well-known phenomenon that a doctoral dissertation gains in authority the moment its author becomes a professor of law.

Aleksander Peczenik, Scientia Juris: Legal Doctrine as Knowledge of Law and as a Source of Law

Foreword

What exactly are *the sources of law*? This is an important question, if only because one of the main responsibilities of a judge in a legal case is to consult whatever sources of law pertain to her particular jurisdiction and to apply whatever relevant norms are found therein. On the face of it the answer to our question is simple and obvious: the relevant sources of law include, paradigmatically: the constitution, any statutes produced by authorized legislative bodies, and (in at least all common law jurisdictions) official reports of cases in which authoritative judicial rulings stand as binding precedents. But this simple answer is far from complete. For one thing, it fails to tell us *why* these are sources of law. Why are statutes a source of law in the United States and Germany but *Hammurabi's Code* is not? Jurisprudential theories will divide on how one is to go about addressing this issue. But the simple answer is incomplete for another, no less important reason. Sometimes judges seek direction from a range of other sources, particularly when the norms derived from the aforementioned standard sources provide insufficient guidance. In at least some legal systems, judges draw on statutes enacted in other jurisdictions. Or they seek guidance in reports of similar cases decided in foreign countries with legal systems and legal cultures similar to their own. Sometimes—indeed more often than most people probably think—judges draw on what respected legal scholars have to say on difficult legal questions. Maybe a highly regarded professor of law has, in analyzing a complex line of decisions, detected an underlying rule or principle at play. Perhaps no individual judge in any particular case was consciously aware of this underlying norm or explicitly invoked it in deciding her case. But the scholar might well have fashioned a convincing argument that commitment to the norm explains and justifies most aspects of the various judicial decisions that were actually made. Commitment to that norm provides those decisions with a kind of coherence hitherto unrecognized. If so, a later judge might cite the scholar's norm when dealing with a new case, one that is not quite the same as those that went before but can arguably be subsumed under the norm that the scholar has identified.

Received wisdom suggests that each of the sources of law discussed in the preceding paragraph falls neatly into one of two mutually exclusive categories. The first group might be called *mandatory sources*. These are such that a judge *must* consult them and *must* apply whatever relevant norms these sources establish. Should these mandatory norms (so understood) fail to provide conclusive guidance because, e.g., they are, on the matter before the court, somewhat vague or inde-terminate, or because they impose conflicting demands, then, and only then, is the judge permitted to consult norms derived from the second category. These we might call *permissive sources*. The norms of foreign jurisdictions or the opinions of legal scholars expressed in their academic commentaries are, according to received wisdom, examples of permissive sources of law. That is, judges are permitted, but not required, to consult them when deciding issues left unresolved by norms derivable from the relevant mandatory sources. Consulting mandatory sources is a matter of judicial duty; consulting permissive sources is a matter of judicial discretion. A judge is legally warranted in consulting permissive sources but she does no wrong, legally speaking, should she fail to do so.

In this groundbreaking exploration and analysis of this standard picture, Fábio Shecaira sets out to establish a third, distinctive category of legal source—what he calls *should-sources*. According to Shecaira, certain forms of legal scholarship can and do count as instances of this third source of law. Unlike mandatory sources, which judges are under duty to consult and which issue norms that must, in all but exceptional circumstances be applied; or permissive sources that judges are not required to use but which, if used reasonably, provide a significantly weaker reason for deciding one way rather than another; a should-source, in Shecaira's words, "should be used and enforced in a sense of 'should' that is fairly strong but not strong enough to count as authoritative"—as is the case with mandatory sources. It would be a serious legal mistake, Shecaira argues, for judges to ignore legal scholarship as a source of law, or to dismiss out of hand the norms articulated in these sources. And to be clear, the argument is not simply that good legal scholarship offers perspicuous descriptions of norms established elsewhere—in, e.g., statutes or court decisions on similar cases. It is that the reflections of legal scholars can be, and indeed in many jurisdictions *are*, a genuine *source* of the norms therein articulated. Legal scholarship can and sometimes does *itself* serve to establish law. It does not merely describe, criticize, or recommend changes to law established elsewhere.

This is a bold, innovative thesis that runs deeply counter to much received thinking on the nature of law. Establishing its bare plausibility, let alone its attractiveness as a view to be eagerly embraced, requires the efforts of a scholar of considerable patience, ingenuity and talent. Fortunately, in Fábio Shecaira one clearly finds such a scholar. There is much in his careful analysis that deserves our serious attention and should cause us to reconsider our views about how judges go about deciding cases. And for that all legal scholars should be truly grateful.

March 2013   W. J. Waluchow

Acknowledgments

This book began as a Ph.D. thesis written in 2011 and defended early in 2012 in the philosophy department of McMaster University. In writing the thesis, and later in turning it into a book, I benefited from the assistance of many friends and colleagues. I am particularly indebted to the following people for their brilliant comments, challenging criticism, and sound advice: Luís Duarte d'Almeida, Richard Fallon, Michael Giudice, Stefan Sciaraffa, Natalie Stoljar, Noel Struchiner, Wil Waluchow (my doctoral supervisor), and an anonymous referee for Springer. Noel and Wil deserve special thanks: they are mentors to whom I constantly turn for guidance in all professional matters. I am also very grateful to my parents, Roseli and Farid, and to my wife, Natália, whose loving support has allowed me to complete this and many other challenging projects.

Contents

Chapter 1
Introduction

1.1 Introduction

This introduction will serve a twofold purpose. First, it will make explicit some of the more contentious theoretical assumptions from which my study of legal scholarship as a source of law departs. As *assumptions*, they will not be directly defended here or in the chapters that follow. But if not directly, they will at least be "indirectly" defended in a sense that will be explained shortly. Second, this introduction will provide a brief sketch of the content of the book.

Let us begin with the assumptions. The basic conceptual equipment of which I will avail myself in giving an account of sources of law in general and of legal scholarship specifically is a conceptual equipment that may be described as "Hartian". I do not endorse (not necessarily because I disagree with, but some-times simply because I wish to remain agnostic about) every specific detail of H. L. A. Hart's jurisprudence. I do endorse, however, what may be regarded as central tenets of Hart's version of legal positivism. For instance, any Hartian must believe that the unity and content of a legal system depend on the existence of a social rule (or perhaps a set of social rules) setting out criteria of legal validity. What makes this rule *social* is the fact that it is sustained by the practices of agents concentrating political power. A related Hartian view that will be taken for granted in this book involves a conceptual association between sources of law and what Hart termed "content-independent" reasons for action (to wit, sources of law are sources of norms that function as content-independent reasons for action). These elliptical remarks will be duly developed in Chaps. 2 and 3, which explain exactly what I understand by the notion of a criterion of legal validity (and how it relates to the notion of a source of law) and provide a detailed account of the often mis-understood notion of content-independence. At this point it suffices to give an initial impression of my theoretical point of departure.

Taking Hart's basic views for granted creates the risk of alienating readers of different jurisprudential persuasions. I make no apology for this. As I will explain later, a study of sources of law is essentially a study of legal (and more specifi-cally, judicial) reasoning. My account of legal scholarship as a source of law

F. P. Shecaira, *Legal Scholarship as a Source of Law*,
SpringerBriefs in Law, DOI: 10.1007/978-3-319-00428-0_1,
© The Author(s) 2013

would be condemned to be disappointingly superficial (if at all informative) if it were to rest on a truly ecumenical, all-embracing account of legal reasoning. To say something worthwhile about the different ways in which judges put legal scholarship to use one simply cannot avoid making some contentious assumptions. I do have the hope, at any rate, that in constructing a plausible and subtle account of legal scholarship as a source of law, I may contribute to making some initially unsympathetic readers friendlier to my jurisprudential assumptions. (That is what was meant earlier by the claim that my assumptions will be "indirectly" defended in the course of this work). Judicial use of legal scholarship is one of the most intricate and elusive aspects of judicial reasoning.[1] Producing a plausible account of this phenomenon while employing a Hartian conceptual framework may be an interesting way of displaying the explanatory potential of that framework. Indeed, given the stagnant stage now reached by the debate between Hartians and their non-positivist opponents, it may pay to pursue an argumentative strategy that, though not novel, has not been used as often or as systematically as it deserves to be. Instead of insisting on conceptual arguments that appear to speak only to the intuitions of their very proponents (think, for instance, of Joseph Raz's famous arguments in defense of exclusive legal positivism, i.e. arguments depending on a contentious analysis of the concept of authority and its relation to the concept of law), we might attempt to breathe new life into the debate by putting the theories under contention to the test of explaining various concrete features of legal practice. Accordingly, this book can be regarded as an attempt to test Hartian positivism by considering whether it can help in the construction of a good account of judicial use of legal scholarship. From this point on I will stop trying explicitly to defend Hartian positivism: I will simply pick up my Hartian conceptual toolbox and get to work. The hope is that the reader who finds persuasive my account of legal scholarship as a source of law will not forget to extend their sympathy for that account to the tools with the aid of which it was constructed.

There is another set of assumptions that should be made explicit. They pertain to methodological questions that might be raised with respect to my somewhat amateurish foray into comparative law. For instance, in Chap. 4 there will be an attempt to provide evidence for a number of claims about the role that scholarship plays in judicial argument by referring to the practices of courts in different jurisdictions. My contention that these different courts exhibit similar practices, a contention made without much regard for the doctrinal differences that are likely

---

[1] In 2011 I had the invaluable opportunity to spend a semester at Harvard Law School as a visiting researcher among academic lawyers with the most diverse backgrounds. The elusiveness mentioned in the text, something in which I have believed for quite some time, was corroborated at Harvard. Everyone willing to discuss the issue seemed to have an opinion about the role that legal scholarship plays in judicial decision-making. But the opinions varied widely from the enthusiastic—"scholarship is extremely important for judges"—to the thoughtful—"scholarship is influential, but its influence is exerted indirectly through concepts and doctrines that are picked up by judges during their training"—to the cynical—"it is said that scholarship is a source of law—but, of course, this is said by scholars".

to exist among diverse legal cultures, may give the reader attuned to debates concerning comparative law methodology the impression that I favor some kind of crude functionalist approach to comparative law. Given the flak that functionalists have received in the past (Michaels 2006), I should note that I am aware of the methodological hazards associated with functionalism. Indeed, if I am a functionalist then I am a functionalist in a weak sense, a sense in which we should all be (and hopefully already are) functionalists. What I mean by this is that while recognizing the importance of doctrine, I worry that excessive emphasis on doctrinal differences between jurisdictions may help to obscure functional similarities. It is common place, for example, that although civilian legal systems often officially reject the doctrine of *stare decisis*, decisions issuing from their courts of appeal tend to be accorded great weight by lower courts (Merryman and Pérez-Perdomo 2007, 47). The doctrinal difference is not irrelevant here (for only where *stare decisis* is adopted are judges under a strict legal obligation to follow precedent) but we cannot allow it to obscure the fact that precedent often plays functionally similar roles in the reasoning of common law and civilian judges.

The same sort of consideration can be applied to the comparative study of the use of legal scholarship by courts of law. Doctrinal differences may be significant but we should not overemphasize them to the point where we risk missing important functional similarities. In Chap. 4 I argue that in several jurisdictions courts treat legal scholarship as a source of content-independent reasons for action. There is very little discussion of doctrinal differences in that chapter simply because these differences are apt to mislead. To give just one example, England was perhaps once a country that doctrinally set it itself apart from other jurisdictions by maintaining a convention against the citation of living authors. This is not a negligible feature of English judicial practice and it tells us something interesting about English legal culture; but its significance can easily be exaggerated. Even when the convention was in force there were certain noted living authors whose opinions seemed to play a role in judicial reasoning that is hardly distinguishable from the role played by scholarly opinions in jurisdictions where jurists are openly regarded as sources of law.

On a related matter, although it is not exactly my intention to debunk an arguably common understanding among comparative lawyers with respect to the importance of the role played by legal scholarship in different legal cultures, some of my conclusions (partly as a result of my functional approach) will be in tension with that common understanding. Take the following as a representative statement of the understanding at issue:

> [T]he main function of the activity of legal theorists, which is responsible for their enormous importance and influence in the development of law in countries of the Continental European tradition, is and has always been that of providing guidance for the administration of justice.... In countries such as those in the "common law" world where juristic works have scant importance – to the point where the idea of a "legal science" is deemed entirely foreign and no legal philosopher is concerned with analyzing its methodology and epistemological presuppositions – this function of providing guidelines for judicial decisions is less often fulfilled, and legal writers and professors are wont to limit themselves to describing and

systematizing the existing legislated and judge-made rules. ... Doubtless this self-limitation
of the activity of Anglo-Saxon jurists is... explained by the tendency that judges in these
countries have to face on their own the theoretical problems that are relevant to their decisions, paying little attention to the recommendations of legal writers.... (Nino 1979, 97–98).

The arguments in Chap. 4 will lead to conclusions that clash more or less
explicitly with Nino's picture. I will not argue against the plausible view that legal
academics have historically enjoyed unequaled prestige in Continental Europe. It
is dubious, however, whether this supports the related but different conclusion that
academic writings are currently more often used *as sources of law* in Continental
Europe than in common law jurisdictions. On the other hand, as indicated in the
endless literature on legal scholarship produced in the United States, it is certainly
false that scholars in common law countries engage predominantly in descriptive,
law-reporting enterprises. It is also false that Anglo-Saxon legal scholars (philosophers included) have utterly ignored the nature of "legal science". American
scholars (although they rarely describe the juristic enterprise as scientific) have
discussed it extensively in recent decades. British scholars (whom Nino may have
had more clearly in mind) have also not ignored legal science. Indeed, my own
understanding of legal scholarship has been influenced by two important philosophical works authored by Britons (Harris 1979; Simmonds 1984). Nino's book is
from 1979, and it is possible that he was roughly right about the state of affairs
obtaining until then. If that is the case, then Nino cannot be accused of making a
mistake, but his picture of the nature of legal scholarship and its influence in the
common law world needs to be updated.

A brief note should be provided about my use of decisions from the Supreme
Court of Canada. The book is interspersed with references to such decisions and I
should be very careful not to give the reader the wrong impression. Canadian
decisions are used merely as means of illustrating very specific points about the
ways in which legal scholarship can (and in Chap. 6, *ought to*) be used. I do not
intend to make bold claims about the status of legal scholarship in Canada as I do
about its status in England, the US, Germany, Scotland, and South Africa. I do
have the impression that the Supreme Court of Canada uses some scholarly
writings as genuine sources of law; but at this point it is just an impression. I have
not done the systematic investigation required to establish that the Court indeed
maintains a convention assigning to certain writings the role of sources of law; I
have looked only at a small number of judgments ranging over an untidy variety of
issues.

Now that some of my substantive and methodological assumptions have been
exposed, I should provide a summary of what is to come in the ensuing chapters.
Before discussing legal scholarship as a source of law, I intend to provide a general
account of sources of law. As Shiner has recently pointed out, this is a concept that
analytic legal philosophers have unfortunately neglected:

The topic of the sources of law is a traditional one in jurisprudence. Yet, remarkably, very
little attention has been paid to the topic in recent analytical jurisprudence. Much contemporary analytical legal theory does not consider the notion of a 'source of law' at all. There is
no entry for the term in the indices of such central contemporary texts as Alexy 1989;

Beyleveld and Brownsword 1986; Dworkin 1978 and 1986; Finnis 1980; MacCormick 1978. Other theorists mention the term and pass on. Raz, for example (see Raz 1979), characterizes his theoretical position as "the sources thesis," that every law has a social source. But he gives relatively little articulation of the concept of a source. Rather, he lays out the implications of such a thesis, leaving the term "source" intuitive and primary (Shiner 2005, 1).

Chapters 2 and 3 will thus be devoted to the task of setting out an account of sources of law. Chapter 2 will not quite provide a definition (in terms of necessary and sufficient conditions) of the concept of a source of law but will roughly establish the boundaries of that concept's extension by indicating what sorts of things qualify as sources of law and what sorts of things do not. One important, and perhaps unusual, feature of my account will be the claim that sources of law are to be distinguished from the norms (i.e. the normative propositions or meaning-contents) that can be derived from those sources. More than the typical English-speaking legal theorist, I take seriously the literal meaning of the phrase "source of law". A source of law is not a law (the kind of normative proposition by which judges allow themselves to be guided) but quite literally something from which law can be derived. Judges looking at the same source (e.g. a section of a statute) may understand it differently and hence disagree about what *law* requires. If the disagreement is reasonable and intractable, then the law is indeterminate: the agreed-upon source of law fails to issue determinate law. The importance of the distinction between source and norm will become clear as I develop my account.

Once a working conception of sources of law is in place, I will explain (and here Hart's influence will start to become clear) why it is that we ought to look to judicial argument in order to determine whether something plays the role of a source of law in a given legal system. In particular, we ought to consider whether judges argue as if they were obligated (in the case of mandatory sources) or as if they had permission (in the case of permissive sources) to invoke the sources of law in question. Chapter 2 will end with a caveat about the potentially misleading character of judicial discourse, and with the related suggestion that the face value of judicial argument is not always a reliable guide to the true nature of judicial reasoning (i.e. to the norms that judges effectively allow themselves to be guided by).

In Chap. 3 I will continue to develop my account of sources of law by associating them with content-independent reasons for action. My understanding of content-independence is roughly Hartian, in the sense that Hart seemed to be aiming at the conception that I provide, although he did not state it as clearly or precisely as he might have. It will be argued that this lack of clarity prompted criticisms of Hart's account that can be avoided once it is made more precise. In the second part of Chap. 3 I will suggest that sources of law are to be regarded as sources of content-independent reasons for action, although not necessarily of peremptory reasons for action. Separating the notions of content-independence and peremptoriness is crucial to understanding an intuitive distinction commonly made by jurists between permissive and mandatory sources of law. Also important for understanding that distinction is a further distinction between *using a source* of law and *applying the legal norm* to be derived from it.

With the conceptual groundwork thus laid, legal scholarship will be the focus of Chap. 4. It will begin by describing the features of the kind of legal scholarship which is most likely to serve the function of a source of law in contemporary legal systems: it is (using terms which will require elucidation) prescriptive, practically oriented, formalist legal scholarship. It is with this specific kind of legal scholarship (not legal scholarship generally) that I will deal in the remainder of the book. In the second part of Chap. 4 I will make a conceptual as well as an empirical argument. The conceptual argument is intended to show that there is no conceptual impediment to scholarship's functioning as a genuine source of law (i.e. a source of content-independent reasons for action). The empirical argument is intended to show that legal scholarship has been used as a source of law in some jurisdictions. It will also be argued, somewhat boldly, that although scholarship is more commonly used as a permissive source of law, there are cases in which it appears to be used as a source producing norms that are very weighty.

In Chap. 5, I will discuss and challenge the assumption sometimes made by comparative lawyers to the effect that judges are more or less disposed to use legal scholarship depending on how eager they are to restrict (or at least *make it seem* as if they were restricting) their ability to exercise discretion. The precise correlation that I will question is one between lack of judicial reference to legal scholarship and a wish to efface from judicial decisions the elements of personal judgment. My argument will require discussion of the intricate connections existing among the use of scholarship, the use of substantive argument, and the exercise of discretion.

In Chap. 6 some normative questions will be addressed pertaining to how and when judges ought to use legal scholarship. My comments will be quite general, having mostly to do with mistakes that those inquiring into normative questions should avoid. The only fairly specific recommendation I am willing to make is that judges in democratic countries ought to use legal scholarship with candor. The claim that they may fail to do so will be illustrated with two decisions issued by the Supreme Court of Canada. (Again, there will be no suggestion that this court *systematically* employs legal scholarship in the objectionable way that they did in those two cases; this claim could only be substantiated by a kind of research which I have not done. To avoid any misunderstanding in this regard, I will also describe a Canadian case in which legal scholarship is used in an exemplary way.)

Finally, to conclude, two things will be done. First, I will summarize the content of the book. Then, I will address some objections (other than those considered within Chaps. 1–6) that may be raised against my account of legal scholarship as a source of law. All these objections, it will be argued, rest on the same type of mistake: namely, that of taking puzzles about sources of law in general to be puzzles that only plague the particular notion of legal scholarship as a source of law. I leave these objections to the end because my answer to them will be more easily articulated once my account of legal scholarship as a source of law is complete.

References

Harris J (1979) Law and legal science: an inquiry into the concepts legal rule and legal system. Clarendon Press, Oxford

Merryman JH, Pérez-Perdomo R (2007) The civil law tradition. An introduction to the legal systems of Europe and Latin America, 3rd edn. Stanford University Press, Stanford

Michaels R (2006) The functional method of comparative law. In: Reimann M, Zimmermann R (eds) The Oxford handbook of comparative law. Oxford University Press, Oxford

Nino CS (1979) Algunos Modelos Metodológicos de "Ciencia" Jurídica. Universidad de Carobobo, Valencia

Shiner R (2005) Legal institutions and the sources of law. Springer, Dordrecht

Simmonds N (1984) The decline of juridical reason: doctrine and theory in the legal order. Manchester University Press, Manchester

Chapter 2
What is a Source of Law?

2.1 Preliminaries

"Source of law" is an ambiguous phrase. It is used variously to refer to: (1) agents (individual officials or institutions) who are authorized to make law; (2) the products resulting from the law-making activities of such agents; (3) interpretive materials that bear on the content of legal norms; and (4) criteria of legal validity operative in a legal system. This list does not exhaust all the possible uses of "source of law" but it is all we need for the moment.[1] I submit that we should use "source of law" to refer to things of the sorts described in (1) and (2) but not to things falling under the descriptions in (3) and (4). By doing so, we avoid some intricate and enduring jurisprudential controversies that are best left untouched.

Legislatures, administrative agencies, and courts are examples of law-making institutions that fit the description in (1). Legislation, precedent, and custom on the other hand are examples of the kinds of things that law-making institutions produce: therefore they fit the description in (2).[2] Thus, "source of law", as I use the term, refers either to a human agent (or an institution composed of human agents) or to the product of that agent's law-making activities. Normally context will allow the reader to discern the specific sense in which I use "source of law", although I will privilege the sense in which it refers to products (as distinct from agents). For the *immediate* sources of legal norms—the things to which judges directly look when attempting to determine what the law is—are things like statutes, judicial decisions, and customary practices.

There is a harmless imprecision in my use of the phrase "source of law" which deserves to be mentioned. This has to do with the fact that the phrase can be used to refer to objects at different levels of generality. For instance, legislation has been given as an example of a source of law, but I would also admit that one can

---

[1] See Vogenauer (2006, 878) and Regla (2000, 21–23) for different and slightly longer lists.

[2] One might object that customs are not exactly *products* of law-making activities, but instead that they are the activities themselves; for customs are social practices that do not necessarily result in documents like statutes and judicial decisions. I would not dispute the point: the distinction between activities and the products thereof is admittedly not razor sharp.

F. P. Shecaira, *Legal Scholarship as a Source of Law*,
SpringerBriefs in Law, DOI: 10.1007/978-3-319-00428-0_2,
© The Author(s) 2013

describe a particular piece of legislation (as opposed to legislation in general) as a source of law; and I would even admit that something as specific as a particular provision in a particular statute can be described as a source of law. The level of generality at which I speak when employing the phrase "source of law" will vary according to context and purpose. For instance, the rule of recognition of a legal system (a notion that will be explained later in this chapter) normally will not make reference to very specific instances of sources of law, e.g. it normally will not direct judges to use and apply *this* or *that* particular precedent. But it also will not direct judges to apply precedents generally, for that would be quite uninformative. Instead, the rule of recognition will normally make prescriptions at an intermediate level of generality, directing judges to use and apply, for instance, the precedents issued by a court of law occupying a specific place in the judicial hierarchy. Thus, whenever I speak of "sources of law" with the intention of referring to sources as they are identified in the rule of recognition of a given legal system, I will be speaking of sources at an intermediate level of generality. On the other hand, when focusing more narrowly on the behavior of a particular court, I may refer to a judge's use of a particular document (e.g. a statute, a case report) as a use of a source of law. Finally, "source of law" will be used in its most general sense in the context of comparative legal analyses: it could be said, for instance, that precedent (without qualification) figures as a mandatory source of law in common law systems but less often in civil law systems.

But this is as much imprecision as our subject allows. In what follows I will argue that the notion of a source of law can only be stretched so far. It is especially important not to confuse the senses of "source of law" accepted here with any of the two further senses associated with (3) and (4). Let us begin with (3).[3] Interpretive materials include anything that a law-applying official may use as a means for discerning the content of a legal norm. Conventions governing the use of technical and non-technical language and *travaux préparatoires* (or any other evidence of authorial intent), for instance, are materials standardly used by judges to discern the meaning of legal texts. Different jurisprudential theories about what it is that gives meaning to a legal text will recommend recourse to different interpretive materials. So, on the view that interpretive materials are sources of law, two judges who approach the same piece of legislation with different interpretive strategies in mind—e.g. one of them focusing on literal meaning, the other on intended meaning—would be described as having recourse to different sources of law. On my view, however, these judges are appealing to the same source of law, namely, a relevant piece of legislation. The judges admittedly treat the same piece of legislation quite differently in that they attempt to identify the norms it establishes in importantly different ways; but they cannot be said to be using different *sources*. My reason for denying the status of sources of law to things

---

[3] This sense of "source of law" is not merely a conceivable one which has been contrived for the purpose of illustration. Indeed, "source of law" has been used in this sense before by Raz (2009, 47–48). More accurately, Raz employs a notion of source of law which is broad enough to encompass interpretive materials *in addition to* the things I describe here as sources of law.

falling under (3) is precisely that it is important to distinguish clearly between sources of law, on the one hand, and means for deriving legal norms from sources, on the other. One who uses "source of law" indiscriminately to refer to the product of the law-making activities of officials and to the materials used for deriving norms from that product risks overlooking a distinction that has significant jurisprudential implications.

Let me give an example of the kind of implication I have in mind. It has been claimed, most famously by Dworkin (1986, Chap. 1) but also, more recently, by several other scholars (Berman 2009; Shapiro 2009; Sciaraffa 2012) that Hartian legal positivism cannot account for the argumentative nature of judicial practice. More precisely, it has been said that the Hartian notion of a rule of recognition is incompatible with the existence of judicial argument about proper interpretive methodology (some judges are textualists, others are intentionalists, others purposivists, etc.). For, in Hart's own words, the rule of recognition is supposed to "specify some feature or features possession of which by a suggested rule is taken as conclusive affirmative indication that it is a rule of [the legal system]" (Hart 1961, 94). Hart's critics claim that the existence of judicial disagreement about interpretive methodology in contemporary legal systems is not easily squared with Hart's view that the rule of recognition (a rule whose existence and content depends on official consensus) *conclusively* identifies valid rules of law in those systems.

Hartian positivists might plausibly answer this objection by claiming that it is based on a mistaken interpretation of Hart's position: for Hart, the rule of recognition has the function of specifying sources of law (in something like my narrower sense) but *not* that of delineating proper interpretive procedures for extracting content from those sources (Berman 2009, 273, note 13). In other words, the rule of recognition tells law-applying officials where to look (statutes, precedents, etc.) but not exactly how to interpret—with what precise interpretive materials—what they are looking at. Hart's account of the rule of recognition, if this interpretation is correct, would thus be shown to be compatible with the existence of judicial argument about proper interpretive methodology simply because the rule of recognition places no specific constraints on judicial interpretive practice.[4] My point is that a broad notion of source like Raz's may help to obscure a distinction that plays an important part in a defense of Hartian positivism against some of its contemporary critics. In light of this, it seems wise (especially

---

[4] I am not quite prepared to endorse this positivist reply to the objection from interpretive disagreement: when Hart speaks of the rule of recognition identifying valid legal *rules* it is not clear to me whether he means *sources* (e.g. a by-law stating that "vehicles are not allowed in the park") or instead the *norms* that are derivable from sources by means of interpretation (e.g. the norm, derived through the literal interpretation of the by-law's text, that vehicles are not to enter the park). Indeed, the best strategy for a Hartian positivist may be to concede that the rule of recognition has the function of prescribing proper interpretive procedures and to argue that, *pace* positivism's critics, contemporary legal systems in fact do contain officially recognized norms about how to interpret sources of law (I develop such an argument myself in Shecaira 2012). Both replies seem to me to hold some promise; I only allude to the first in the text in order to illustrate the importance of the distinction at issue.

to positivists but also to anyone genuinely interested in understanding Hart's legal theory) to simply avoid treating interpretive materials as sources of law.

What about (4)?[5] According to Hart, criteria of legal validity are conditions whose fulfillment by a rule guarantees its validity or, in other words, its bindingness within a legal system. (These and other Hartian concepts will be explained in more detail shortly). Some authors have understood the notion of criteria of validity in a way that approximates it to my understanding of sources of law. Gardner, for instance, has defined the Hartian rule of recognition, the rule which specifies criteria of legal validity, as "a norm that identifies some person or institution as an ultimate (i.e., non-delegated) maker of law" (Gardner 2007, 61, footnote omitted). If this is how criteria of validity are to be understood, as picking out the agents who are authorized to make law, then I am happy to identify sources of law with the sorts of things falling under (4). The problem however is that Gardner's account is not uncontroversial. Hart himself seemed to believe that the rule of recognition can do more than Gardner allows, such as placing constraints—even moral constraints (Hart 1994, 250)—on the kinds of norms that can be issued by persons or institutions identified as ultimate makers of law. So, for Hart, criteria of validity include requirements that qualify as specifications of sources of law in my sense (e.g. the requirement that a norm be issued by parliament) but they also include requirements that should be described as imposing constraints on the content of the law (e.g. the requirement that parliament's acts respect individual rights and freedoms).[6] The upshot is that denying the complete identification of sources of law with criteria of legal validity is a way of avoiding an enduring controversy about the correct understanding of the latter notion. Meanwhile nothing is lost or risked by keeping separate the notions of a source of law and that of a constraint on the content of the law.

The attentive reader will have noticed that morality (i.e. substantive, critical moral theory) has not been mentioned as one of the possible candidates for the status of sources of law.[7] This might motivate the conclusion (and perhaps the worry) that at this preliminary stage sources of law are defined in a way that reveals my positivist inclinations. While it is true that I have such inclinations, they are not exerting significant influence at this early stage. Sources of law, as the term is most often employed here, are things (e.g. documents and practices) from which norms (i.e.

---

[5] At times Hart (1961, 103, 1982, 260) used "source of law" and "criterion of legal validity" as synonyms.

[6] Note that these are not specific interpretive constraints to the effect that legal texts ought to be read literally or purposively or in some other way. While it is fairly uncontroversial that Hart believed that the rule of recognition could (and often did) place general moral constraints on the content of legal norms, it is not clear (as I mentioned earlier) whether more specific instructions about interpretive methodology would also be included in the rule of recognition.

[7] An important reason for proceeding in this way will appear in Chap. 3, when I associate sources of law with content-independent reasons for action. This association, as noted in the introduction, is a contentious one likely to be readily accepted only by positivists. In what follows, however, I will explain that my narrow notion of a source of law, apart from its association with content-independent reasons, is not a product of narrow positivist sympathies.

normative propositions or meaning-contents) are derivable. Critical morality, on the other hand, is itself a set of normative propositions whose source varies according to one's metaethics: e.g. propositions of critical morality may have their source in intuition or in rational reflection. For this simple reason it would be inaccurate to characterize critical morality as a *source* of law. Notice that this is not a positivist argument: denying morality the status of a source of law is not to deny its importance to legal reasoning. Indeed, I start off with a working conception of sources of law that is probably acceptable to most contemporary philosophers of law, to non-positivists like Dworkin and even to most natural lawyers.

Consider Dworkin, one of whose central ambitions has been to demonstrate that legal reasoning cannot be dissociated from moral reasoning. Dworkin's concerns can easily be accommodated by a provisional acceptance of the view that moral norms may be counted among the interpretive materials that bear on the content of legal norms. Although his earlier work might suggest otherwise (Dworkin 1977, 40-1), Dworkin's later work (1986, Chap. 7) is plausibly understood as a defense of the view that positive law must be read by law-appliers in the light of moral principles; the content of legal norms cannot be settled simply by reference to the actions and intentions of human agents but also requires reference to principles of critical morality that explain and justify the products of such actions and intentions. On this reading, Dworkin understands moral norms as necessary aids to the interpretation of law, as a necessary part of the strategy that law-appliers must use in order to derive legal norms from sources of law. I do not wish to quarrel with this view at this point: morality might indeed play a central role in legal reasoning but the role it would play is still not that of a *source* of law (as I have defined the notion).

As to natural lawyers, they too could probably accept my narrow account of sources of law. Contemporary natural lawyers vehemently reject the view that "a norm's status as a correct moral norm is sufficient for its being a legal norm" (Murphy 2003, 242). Some of them even deny that moral validity is always necessary for legal validity (ibid., 243, footnote 15). That being the case, all that natural lawyers maintain is that moral correctness can function as a necessary condition for legal validity. But, again, so far my account of sources of law has not denied this possibility; all it says is that conditions of legal validity ought not invariably to be understood as *sources* of law.

To recapitulate: the upshot of this section is that things falling under (1) and (2) can be understood as sources of law while things falling under (3) and (4) should not be so understood. So far I have given just a few examples of things falling under (1) and (2): legislatures, courts of law, and administrative agencies; legislation, judicial precedent, and custom. It is not necessary, for the purposes of this study, to list and discuss all the examples of sources of law that are relevant to modern legal systems.[8] However, some brief remarks about the examples given so far are in order.

---

[8] For a comprehensive account of sources of law and of the intricate ways in which they interact in common law and civil law systems, see Shiner (2005). For the objection that Shiner's account is not comprehensive enough, see Guastini (2007). Shiner replies in Shiner (2007).

First, I use "legislation" in a very broad sense. Constitutions, as well as statutes, are examples of legislation for my purposes. General norms created by bodies whose law-making power is delegated by legislatures (e.g. regulatory agencies) are also included here. One distinctive and important feature of legislation is that the norms it contains are expressed in words that in modern legal systems are accorded canonical status. Unlike the expressed rationale for a judicial decision, which does not have canonical force, the words of a statute or a constitution are not subject to modification and are not otherwise transparent to their underlying justification. (Here Dworkin and some natural lawyers might understandably begin to wince.)

Second, judicial precedent can be a source of law even where the doctrine of *stare decisis* is not officially in force (Gardner 2007, 74). The doctrine of *stare decisis* makes judicial decisions binding on other courts, and sometimes even on the same court in the future. But where precedent does not officially bind, one may still characterize it as a source of law so long as it plays at least a "persuasive" role in judicial argument (I will say more about the notion of a persuasive source of law, and will explain my reluctance to use the term "persuasive", in Chap. 3).

Third, when I refer to custom in this book I will usually have *official* custom in mind, that is, I will be referring to the convergent practices of judges or other law-making and law-applying agents. This is neither to say that the customs of legal subjects cannot be sources of law nor that they are unimportant where they do function as sources of law.[9]

Much has been said about "sources" but not much about "law". For the moment, only a couple of points are necessary. First, I restrict my use of "sources of law" to refer to sources of general legal norms as opposed to individual legal norms. So: *One must pay one's contractually acquired debts* is an instance of a general norm while *Smith must give Jones 50 dollars in accordance with the terms of the contract to which they assented* is an example of an individual norm. Both kinds of norms can be legal norms but only those of the general kind are *laws*. Admittedly, this is more stipulation than anything else; but it is a fairly common stipulation the adoption of which will help to avoid confusion.

Second, for something to be a source of law in a given legal system it need not (although it commonly does) issue norms that *belong to* that legal system. For instance, a legal system (through its rules of so-called private international law) may determine that cases with certain international connections be regulated by foreign law. That system thereby recognizes the validity, or the bindingness, of foreign law with respect to the relevant cases, but it does not *ipso facto* incorporate the foreign legal norms. Foreign legislation, for instance, can function as a source of law in cases with international connections even though the norms it yields will remain a part of foreign, not domestic, law. The upshot is that by "source of law" I

---

[9] See Bederman (2010) for an argument to the effect that unofficial customs function "as a source of obligation in contemporary legal cultures and [remain] a potent jurisprudential source, for both domestic polities and international law" (ibid., ix).

mean "source of valid (or binding) law", and the validity of a law does not entail its membership in the system where it is deemed valid.

Two final remarks are in order. First, at the risk of boring the reader, it might pay to emphasize a general point that has already been made. I make a distinction, which legal philosophers often fail to make, between sources of law and legal norms generated by those sources.[10] This entails that different norms can be derived from the exact same source (e.g. a statutory provision) if, for instance, different interpretive methods are employed. This distinction may seem pedantic, but it is related to my criticism of Raz's understanding of sources of law, and it will also play a significant role in Chap. 3 (with respect to the distinction made there between *use* and *enforcement*).

Finally, the title of this book implies that I regard legal scholarship as an alternative source of law in addition to the standard examples mentioned so far (namely, legislation, precedent, and custom). That is true, but before we can get to legal scholarship there are many concepts that need to be explained and distinctions that need to be made.

2.2 Sources of Law and Judicial Argument

To determine whether something is a source of law and precisely how it functions in a given legal system, one must look to how judges of that system justify their decisions. There is more to something being a source of law (and to its functioning in a particular way) than the fact that (and the way in which) judges appeal to it in their arguments. But whatever else might be of relevance, playing a part in judicial argument is crucial for something to qualify as a source of law.

This is the point at which my positivist sympathies will definitely come to the surface, as I will be drawing heavily on Hart's theory of law. The Hartian rule of recognition—i.e. the rule specifying criteria by which the bindingness of putative legal norms is to be assessed in a legal system—is best understood as a customary norm (Gardner 2007, 61–66).[11] The rule of recognition depends on the existence of an official practice of treating as binding within the legal system the norms that satisfy certain criteria. Only where officials regard themselves as having an obligation to enforce the norms that satisfy such criteria is it possible to speak of the existence of a rule of recognition. (It will be suggested later that this standard description of the rule of recognition is especially suited to account for mandatory sources of law, given that it refers to *binding* norms that officials have an

---

[10] For discussion as to why the distinction is often ignored and for arguments to the effect that it should not be ignored, see Shecaira (in press).

[11] This view may be challenged by those who regard the rule of recognition as a conventional norm. Good reasons for rejecting the conventionalist understanding of the rule of recognition can be found in Green (1999), Dickson (2007), and Toh (2010).

obligation to enforce. To account for non-mandatory sources, I will need to modify this description slightly but significantly.)

Hart made it clear that different officials are involved in the practice that constitutes the rule of recognition (Hart 1961, 104–107, 117). As Jeffrey Golds-worthy has aptly put it, the relevant practice involves "senior officials of all branches of government" (Goldsworthy 2007, 235). When senior officials of different branches seriously disagree about criteria of legal validity, the rule of recognition lacks determinateness (not entirely, but only in respect of the issue(s) under contention). The point that needs to be stressed here is that judges are invariably among the officials whose practices matter in this regard. Just imagine the uncertainty that would be created by a situation in which the highest courts of a country establish by their own decisions (otherwise deemed proper sources of law), but against the protests of the national legislature, that they, the courts, are empowered to strike down or modify the effects of statutes that violate individual rights and freedoms. The validity of statutes struck down or modified by the courts' decisions on that basis would be uncertain.

The idea that a norm is not legally valid if judges do not regard it as passing the proper tests is an important part of Hart's theory, but it is certainly more than just some Hartian idiosyncrasy. Indeed, that idea is also behind the plausible distinc-tion between law and convention that is made today by many constitutional scholars. Constitutional conventions (as distinct from constitutional law) are regarded as political standards that regulate the relations between certain gov-ernmental persons or institutions. Some standard examples drawn from Com-monwealth nations include the relations between Crown and Parliament, Cabinet and Prime Minister, and the two Houses of Parliament (Marshall 1984, 4). What explains the failure of these standards to count as laws is precisely that they are not enforced (and, perhaps more controversially, not *enforceable*) by courts of law. To be sure, the existence of constitutional conventions has been acknowledged by courts, and conventions have even been used by judges as interpretive aids.[12] But—and this makes all the difference—judges do not regard themselves as being required to apply conventions directly.

The point, once more, is that judges (senior judges at least) are among the officials whose assent is necessary for the existence of a determinate rule of recognition setting out criteria of validity. As I explained earlier, although sources of law are not to be unqualifiedly equated with criteria of legal validity, some criteria of legal validity can indeed be understood as specifying proper sources of law (while others should be understood as imposing constraints on the content of legal norms to be derived from proper sources). For instance, criteria of legal validity which identify certain agents as law-makers can be understood as speci-fying proper sources of law. What follows from these claims—i.e. that judicial

---

[12] Conventions may help to clarify the meaning of the law by "helping to elucidate the background against which legislation took place, thus providing guidance as to the intention of the legislature where the meaning of a statute ha[s] come into question" (Marshall 1984, 15).

assent is crucial for the determinateness of the criteria of legal validity, and that some criteria of validity specify sources of law—is that judicial practice helps determine what counts as a source of law in a legal system. An agent and what he produces are not sources of law if judges refuse to recognize them as such.

Let me move on to a different, but related, issue. It was said earlier that the existence of a rule of recognition depends on judges finding themselves obligated to apply norms which the rule recognizes as binding. I will later relax this requirement by admitting the possibility of non-mandatory sources of law. What matters for the time being is that judges regard criteria of legal validity, including those that specify proper sources of law, as standards by which they should guide their actions. In other words, judges have a *normative* attitude with respect to criteria specifying sources of law. It should also be emphasized that judges tend to express this attitude publicly; they regard criteria of validity "as common standards of official behavior and appraise critically their own and each other's deviations as lapses" (Hart 1961, 113).

There is a traditional jurisprudential distinction between formal and material sources of law (ibid., 246–247). The latter include any factor that causally influences judicial decision-making. The fact that a norm was enacted by a legislature can certainly cause a judge to decide a case in a particular way (i.e. in accordance with the prescriptions of the legislature). But something as trivial as, say, the arrogance of an advocate can also influence a judge by leading him to regard that counsel's case with less sympathy.[13] These two facts can both be regarded as material sources of law insofar as they have significant and systematic impact on the behavior of judges. What these facts usually fail to have in common, however, is that only the first one is associated with a common standard of official behavior. Even when a judge is conscious that the personality of an advocate has an influence over his opinion it is unlikely that he will regard it as the sort of factor that can ground a standard of behavior by which he and his peers should guide their decisions. It seems unlikely that a judge would say or even think something to this effect: "Fellow judges, let us treat a counsel's arrogance as a reason to decide against the party he represents".

Thus, "source of law" in this book invariably means "formal source of law." Where legislation, for instance, is a formal source of law, judges consider themselves duty-bound to use it. It is very important that I restrict my use of "source of law" in this way; for otherwise this book's project might be confused with projects like that of Neil Duxbury in *Jurists and Judges—An Essay on Influence* (2001). In that book Duxbury is primarily concerned with investigating whether and to what extent legal scholarship causally influences judicial decision-making. I on the other hand want to discuss legal scholarship as a formal source of law, i.e. as a

---

[13] Less trivial examples of factors which exert causal influence over law-applying officials but do not usually qualify as formal sources of law are views disseminated by the media, views expressed by private organizations, the intentions of government and other political agents, values widely accepted in civil society, and views expressed by international organizations lacking the formal authorization of international law (Peczenik 2005, 14).

source with regard to which judges maintain specific normative attitudes. At different points in the book reference will be made to Duxbury's findings in his work on juristic influence. This shows that our projects are related in important ways, but it certainly does not show that they are identical.

On a quick note, the distinction between formal and material sources of law was presented above as a traditional one. This should be qualified with the (by this point unsurprising) claim that I have actually given the traditional distinction a Hartian flavor which may not agree with the tastes of all those who endorse the distinction in more general terms. Regla defines a formal source of law as the object of study of those who treat sources of law "as a problem that is internal to the legal order and who, as a consequence, only take into consideration the legal factors... on which the creation of legal norms depends." (2000, 40, my translation) Notice that Regla's account of formal sources is more general than the Hartian one that I present; for Hart develops the notion of something being *internal* to law in a distinctive and somewhat controversial way. Hart refers in his account of criteria of legal validity to social and psychological facts about officials which may vex legal theorists who pursue some Kelsenian ideal of jurisprudential purity. So, while I allude to the traditional concept of a formal source of law, some of the adherents to that tradition may feel alienated insofar as I explain formal sources as sources that are specified as such in a rule constituted by social/psychological facts.

2.3 A Caveat

I do not want to sound naive. When I say that we must look to judicial argument in order to determine the status of a putative source of law, I do not ignore the hazards involved in taking judicial discourse at face value. For one thing, as suggested earlier, the policies of other governmental agents may also affect the status of a putative source of law: the matter is not always settled simply by what judges have to say. Moreover, even where there is no apparent tension between judges and other officials, one must keep in mind that judicial discourse is not always entirely transparent. Ignorance of important historical facts about judicial behavior and excessive focus on a limited set of decisions pertaining to high profile cases can lead to mistaken or skewed analyses. Let me explain what I have in mind.

One important thing to note is that judges can be coy about making reference to certain sources of law, even to sources with regard to which they hold the appropriate normative attitude. At times the divergence between the practice and the rhetoric of judges can grow to a point where judicial attitude can only be characterized as ambiguous, and hence the status of the putative source of law can only be described as unsettled. Judicial attitude in relation to legal scholarship is often elusive in this way. Consider a couple of examples.

Duxbury tells us that in France legal scholarship, particularly in the form of case note writing, has long been influential (2001, Chap. 4). But interestingly citation to academic commentators by judges is a more recent, and still growing, phenomenon in that country. Duxbury associates lack of citation to scholarship in France with the formality and terseness of the opinions written by French judges. Italy also presents an interesting case:

> In contemporary Italy… the legislature has told the courts that they may not cite books or articles in their opinions. Therefore, Italian judges, who are heavily influenced by legal scholarship, employ the ideas suggested to them by scholars without citing them, and refer in a very general way to 'the doctrine,' which is the civil law term for books and articles written by legal scholars (Merryman and Pérez-Perdomo 2007, 59).

The cases of France and Italy are not identical. Italian judges avoid citing particular works of scholars in order to comply with a command issued by the legislature. This does not entirely prevent judges from using scholarship as a source of law, as the legislature's policy is circumvented by the practice of making vague references to "the doctrine". On the other hand, were the Italian legislature to prohibit any reference whatsoever to scholarship by judges, then we might have a case, like most cases where officials of different branches bump heads about criteria of legal validity, in which the status of scholarship as a source of law would be indeterminate. (Indeterminateness would of course also arise if judges themselves were deeply divided about the status of legal scholarship as a source of law).

In France the curiosity arises out of the fact that judicial discourse (i.e. the lack of citation or even loose reference to scholarship) does not reflect judicial practice (i.e. the fact that judges normally look to legal scholarship for inspiration and probably accord more weight to arguments of lawyers that are capable of using scholarly opinions in their favor). This complicates a bit our assessment of the status of legal scholarship in France. But as long as French judges do not explicitly deny that scholarship has a part to play in their reasoning, it cannot be ruled out that they treat scholarship as a genuine source of law. That is to say, lack of reference to scholarship in decisions that are already curt to begin with is not strong evidence against the view that French judges in fact believe that they have reason to decide in accordance with the recommendations of scholars. There apparently is, according to Duxbury, historical evidence indicating that judges indeed resort to scholarship in their reasoning (and apparently expect counsel to use scholarship in their arguments); their attitudes toward scholarship simply do not appear clearly in their written decisions.

My purpose is certainly not to analyze in detail the practices of judges in France or Italy or any other particular country. I rely somewhat uncritically on the reports of other authors because I am more eager to make a general methodological point than to engage in actual comparative legal analysis. The point is that judges may have the appropriate normative attitude with respect to a source of law and yet fail to disclose it fully or unambiguously in their decisions.

Now, even where there is no tension between judges and other officials, and where judges are quite outspoken, judicial discourse should still be dealt with very carefully. Focus on exceptional, high profile decisions is one common source of error. There is a helpful example which is not about sources of law but rather about interpretive methodology. The lesson it provides, however, is generalizable.

American scholars sometimes refer to *Riggs v. Palmer* in order to make jurisprudential points about judicial interpretive practice in the US. In *Riggs*, the Court of Appeals of New York did not allow the defendant, Palmer, to inherit under the will of his grandfather whom he had murdered. The court came to this decision in spite of the fact that the plain meaning of the relevant statutes did not invalidate the grandfather's will. One thing that has been said about *Riggs* is that the decision exhibited a fundamental disagreement within the court about proper interpretive methodology. More precisely, it has been claimed that while the majority allowed the norm flowing from the plain meaning of the statutes to be overridden by a substantive, unwritten principle ("no man may profit from his own wrong"), Judge Gray, the author of the dissenting opinion, stated clearly that "the legislature has, by its enactments, prescribed exactly when and how wills may be made, altered and revoked, and, apparently... has left no room for the exercise of an equitable jurisdiction by courts over such matters" (22 NE 188 (NY 1889), 519).

I am tempted, however, to classify the argument in *Riggs* not as a deep dispute about proper interpretive methodology but as a more superficial one about whether the circumstances in *Riggs* were grave enough to allow for the defeat of the applicable statutes (this notion of defeat will be discussed again in the following chapter). Skepticism about my understanding of *Riggs* may be motivated by Gray's explicit defense of indefeasible literalism in the quoted passage. The skeptics should be encouraged, however, to redirect their skepticism to Gray's rhetoric, whose sincerity is far from certain. As Leiter points out, in *Bockes v. Temple*, a case handed down on the very same day as *Riggs*, Gray seems to have abandoned his literalism: "It is an elementary rule that statutes are to be interpreted according to their intent. The intention of the legislature is undoubtedly the great principle which controls the office of interpretation...;" and he qualifies that by saying that "[i]t is only where the literal acceptation of the words used will work a mischief, or some absurd result, or where some obscurity in the sense compels it, that we need resort to extrinsic aids of interpretation." (cited in Leiter 2009, 1433). It is, thus, either the case that Gray had inconsistent views about interpretation or that he accepted the defeasibility of the plain meaning of statutory law in very special circumstances and simply did not think that *Riggs* provided such circumstances. The latter option finds some support in the fact that Gray states in *Riggs* that "public policy" did not mandate a ruling against Palmer, since he was already being punished for his crime (22 NE 188 (NY 1889) at 519). This suggests that Gray did not see the result in favor of Palmer as absurd or mischievous.

Riggs and similar cases have also been used in defense of the bolder and more general view that American interpretive practice is not rule-governed, i.e. that

American judges are quite free to resort to substantive considerations in the justification of their decisions. All this is said because the court did not apply a statute which was inconsistent with a moral principle. The myopia that afflicts this view is readily perceived when *Riggs* is compared with a series of American cases dealing with very similar questions:

> We can find numerous examples of courts allowing killers to take property that became available to them solely because of their own culpable actions, including cases involving a killer of the testator who was found not guilty by reason of insanity, a killer of the testator who was convicted of voluntary manslaughter, murderers whose acts of murder caused property to pass to their children although not directly to themselves, a murderer convicted of being an accessory after the fact but not of actually wielding the murder weapon, a murderer who did not kill a "testator" but instead as remainderman killed the holder of the life estate… In all of these cases, all falling only slightly short of first and second degree murder, courts have allowed culpable killers to inherit, and have treated the *Riggs v. Palmer* principle, whether embodied in a statute or in the common law, as an exception to be construed narrowly, notwithstanding the broad potential implications of the "no man may profit from his own wrong" principle (Schauer 2004, 1937–1938, footnotes omitted).

Once more, the pattern that suggests itself is that American judges are not willing to deviate from the plain meaning of an applicable statute unless the result which it prescribes is very objectionable. The idea, whose force cannot be appreciated by those who only read *Riggs* and nothing else, is that there is a broad interpretive rule permitting the defeat of a statute's plain meaning only in exceptional cases.

Let me conclude this section by saying that judicial argument remains one of the most important sources of information as to the status of a putative source of law. That does not mean, however, that the text of judicial opinions should always be taken at face value. Analyses of decisions should be systematic (the broader the analysis the more likely it is that inconsistencies will be flagged and broad patterns discerned), and analysts must not ignore the positions of other officials[14] nor historical facts that may illuminate aspects of judicial behavior which judges themselves fail fully to disclose in their decisions.

References

Bederman D (2010) Custom as a source of law. Cambridge University Press, New York

Berman M (2009) Constitutional theory and the rule of recognition: toward a fourth theory of law. In: Himma K, Adler M (eds) The rule of recognition and the U.S. constitution. Oxford University Press, New York

Dickson J (2007) Is the rule of recognition really a conventional rule? Oxford J Legal Stud 27:373

---

[14] For example, in some jurisdictions it can be helpful to look to the conclusions of advocates-general in order to determine what judges regard as good reasons for deciding. See, for instance, Mak (2011, 445) on the use of the conclusions of advocates-general as a source of evidence regarding the influence of foreign precedent on the Dutch Supreme Court.

Duxbury N (2001) Jurists and judges: an essay on influence. Hart Publishing, Oxford

Dworkin R (1977) Taking rights seriously. Duckworth, London

Dworkin R (1986) Law's empire. Harvard University Press, Cambridge

Gardner J (2007) Some types of law. In: Edlin D (ed) Common law theory. Cambridge University Press, New York

Goldsworthy J (2007) The myth of the common law constitution. In: Edlin D (ed) Common law theory. Cambridge University Press, New York

Green L (1999) Positivism and conventionalism. Can J Law Jurisprud 12:35

Guastini R (2007) On the theory of legal sources. A continental point of view. Ratio Juris 20:302

Hart HLA (1961) The concept of law. Clarendon Press, Oxford

Hart HLA (1982) Commands and authoritative reasons. In: Hart HLA (ed) Essays on Bentham: jurisprudence and political theory. Oxford University Press, New York

Hart HLA (1994) The concept of law, 2nd edn. Clarendon Press, Oxford

Leiter B (2009) Explaining theoretical disagreement. Univ Chicago Law Rev 76:1215

Mak E (2011) Why do Dutch and UK judges cite foreign law? Camb Law J 70:420

Marshall G (1984) Constitutional conventions. The rules and forms of political accountability. Clarendon Press, Oxford

Merryman JH, Pérez-Perdomo R (2007) The civil law tradition. An introduction to the legal systems of Europe and Latin America, 3rd edn. Stanford University Press, Stanford

Murphy M (2003) Natural law jurisprudence. Legal Theor 9:241

Peczenik A (2005) Scientia Juris: legal doctrine as knowledge of law and as a source of law. Springer, Dordrecht

Raz J (2009) The authority of law. Essays on law and morality, 2nd edn. Oxford University Press, New York

Regla JA (2000) Teoría General de las Fuentes del Derecho (y del Orden Jurídico). Ariel, Barcelona

Schauer F (2004) The limited domain of law. Va Law Rev 90:1909

Sciaraffa S (2012) Explaining theoretical disagreement and massive decisional agreement: the justificatory view. Problema 6: 165

Shapiro S (2009) What is the rule of recognition (and does it exist)? In: Himma K, Adler M (eds) The rule of recognition and the U.S. constitution. Oxford University Press, New York

Shecaira F (2012) Dealing with judicial rhetoric: a defence of Hartian positivism. Aust J Legal Philos 37:131

Shecaira F (in press) Sources of law are not legal norms. Ratio Juris

Shiner R (2005) Legal institutions and the sources of law. Springer, Dordrecht

Shiner R (2007) Strictly institutionalized sources of law: some further thoughts. Ratio Juris 20:310

Toh K (2010) The predication thesis and a new problem about persistent fundamental legal controversies. Utilitas 22:331

Vogenauer S (2006) Sources of law and legal method in comparative law. In: Reinmann M, Zimmermann R (eds) The Oxford handbook of comparative law. Oxford University Press, New York

Chapter 3
Sources and Reasons

3.1 Authoritative Reasons

Hart believed that legal requirements and authoritative prescriptions more generally provide (or rather are treated as providing)[1] practical reasons with two distinct
characteristics: they are content-independent and peremptory (1982, 253–4, 260).
Hart defined content-independence as a reason's ability to operate "independently
of the nature or character of the action to be done" (ibid., 254). Peremptoriness on
the other hand has to do with a reason's ability to "preclude or cut off any
independent deliberation [by the agent to whom the reason applies] of the merits
pro and con of doing the act" (ibid. 253). I believe Hart was essentially on the right
track but that his account of the two defining features of authority is in need of
some refinement and clarification.

Let us begin with content-independence. Although fairly popular, the Hartian
account of content-independence has generated some skepticism (Markwick 2003;
Sciaraffa 2009). One important source of concern is that Hart's definition of
content-independence is under-inclusive with regard to paradigmatic cases of
content-independent reasons. Sciaraffa (ibid. 236) has given the following example: imagine that the captain of a ship commands a sailor to swab the deck. This
command, issued by an authority to his subordinate, is a paradigmatic example of
a content-independent reason for action. Yet part of the nature or character of the
action commanded is precisely that it responds to the captain's command.
Describing content-independent reasons as reasons that apply independently of the
nature or character of the relevant action would lead us counter-intuitively to
classify the captain's command as a content-*dependent* reason for action; for the

---

[1] Whenever I speak of sources "providing" and of norms "functioning as" reasons for action in
the course of this book, the reader should understand me as making a claim about the role that
sources and norms play in the practical deliberations of the relevant agents. Like Hart, my main
purpose is not to make normative claims about the reasons that are in fact supplied by legal
norms. My purpose is instead to understand legal reasoning as it is performed by legal officials,
especially judges. That involves determining what judges generally *regard* as reasons for action;
whether their normative attitudes are warranted or not is a different issue which is not explored
here in any detail. Chapter 6 will be the only exception to an otherwise non-normative enterprise.

F. P. Shecaira, *Legal Scholarship as a Source of Law*,
SpringerBriefs in Law, DOI: 10.1007/978-3-319-00428-0_3,
© The Author(s) 2013

reason's presence depends on the action having the nature or character of being responsive to the captain's command.

With counter-examples like the command of the captain in mind, Sciaraffa has proposed a reformulation of the notion of content-independence. For him, content-independent reasons should be understood, not as reasons that are independent of the nature or character of the action to be done, but rather as *intentions*. More precisely, Sciaraffa maintains that "an agent has a content-independent reason to ϕ if and only if someone's intent that she ϕ is a reason for her to ϕ" (ibid. 234). The major virtue of Sciaraffa's account is that, unlike Hart's, it appears to be capable of vindicating our intuitions about the application of the concept of content-independence to central cases like that of the captain's command.

However, associating content-independence with intention may generate some uncomfortable theoretical problems. For instance, it is hard to see how Sciaraffa's account could help us to explain the authoritativeness of norms which, to use Gardner's phrase, are authoritative in reception albeit not in creation. A norm that is authoritative in creation is based on "an attempt to change another's normative position by that very act of attempting to change it" (Gardner 2007, 76). Norms that are not intentionally created, i.e. which are not based on any deliberate attempt to effect normative change, can only be authoritative in reception (if authoritative at all). To be clear, Sciaraffa's primary purpose in his paper is not to provide a general account of authority but only an account of content-independence. However, on the assumption that content-independence is a necessary feature of authority, I submit that we need an account of content-independence that coheres with our beliefs about the different ways in which norms (especially legal norms) can be authoritative.

Customary norms are Gardner's prime examples of norms that are not intentionally made (ibid. 63). In the previous chapter the Hartian rule of recognition itself was characterized as a customary rule. The rule of recognition is created by officials in the course of their law-applying activities. For instance, judges enforce and see themselves as bound to enforce bills approved by the legislature. The rule of recognition, i.e. the rule recognizing among other things bills approved by the legislature as binding, is created as a by-product of the official practice of enforcing bills approved by the legislature. Judges do not intend to create the rule of recognition. They simply follow it, and by following it they create it. Other customary legal norms[2] are also the unintended by-products of official practice. An agent's reason to comply with an authoritative customary norm can hardly be associated with someone's intent that they comply; for the relevant intent simply does not exist.

Moreover, from the point of view of the subjects of legal norms, even when the law is intentionally created, it is implausible to claim that they *always* treat the law as authoritative because they take someone's intention as a reason for compliance.

---

[2] To be sure, Hart expressed doubt about whether the rule of recognition itself should be classified as a *legal* rule or not (1961, 108).

It appears that citizens sometimes view themselves as owing allegiance, not to officials or other determinate agents, but to an impersonal set of prescriptions which they vaguely describe as "the law".

Sciaraffa's account of content-independence cannot be deemed faulty just yet. A potential response to the concerns expressed above is suggested by an aspect of Sciaraffa's account which has not yet been mentioned. Sciaraffa affirms that the notion of intention to which he appeals is a broad one, including "not only actual persons' actual intentions, but also actual persons' represented (but not actual) intentions...." (Sciaraffa 2009, 249). In private conversation Sciaraffa suggested to me a parallel between his account of content-independence and Raz's famous contention that only norms which express or *can be represented as* expressing someone's judgment about how others should act are capable of being authoritative. Here Raz defends the view that represented judgments or intentions can do the job (the example he uses being particularly apposite): "[Custom] is not normally generated by people intending to make law. But it can hardly avoid reflecting the judgment of the bulk of the population on how people in the relevant circumstances should act" (1985b, 306). Similarly, Sciaraffa might say that, although customary norms are not actually intentionally created, they may be represented as so being. A customary norm may provide a content-independent reason for action that consists in a represented intention that the norm's subjects abide by it. To be clear, Sciaraffa is not claiming simply that content-independent reasons are either actual intentions or things that can, but might not actually, be represented as intentions. For something to play the role of a content-independent reason it must either *be* an actual intention or *be represented* as such.

This reply is not satisfactory. It leaves unanswered the crucial question of *who* represents the relevant intention in the case of customary legal norms (or, in Raz's terms, the question of who takes customary legal norms to reflect the judgment of the bulk of the population). Given that customary norms are created unintentionally, their creators would only be able to represent the norms as reflecting their intentions once the norms had been created. But by then the authoritativeness of the norms should already have been established. For if instead the authoritative status of the norms depended on pronouncements by (say) judges to the effect that they intend that the norms be obeyed, then their very status as *customary* would be threatened. We do not regard norms which gain authoritative status by means of official judicial pronouncements as customary but rather as part of case law. Customary norms are distinctive precisely in that their force depends simply on their being followed (with the appropriate attitude or, as some might say, with *opinio juris*) by certain agents for an appropriate period of time.

The alternative to this would be to say that the relevant intention is represented, not by the norm's creators, but by those to whom it applies (a group which might include the norm's creators albeit in a different capacity). But this also does not seem to work. Although the subjects of a customary norm might indeed regard it as a reflection of someone's intention or judgment, there is no reason to suppose that the norm's authoritativeness depends on their doing so. As I mentioned earlier, subjects may see themselves as bound by impersonal legal norms.

The upshot is that the notion of content-independence that results from Sciaraffa's reformulation appears to be of limited usefulness to the analysis of legal authority. It does not seem that legal authority exists only where the intent (actual or represented) that a legal subject φ is a reason for her to φ. To be clear, these concerns about Sciaraffa's account of content-independence do not establish that it is useless; indeed, it may still be helpful to those interested in the analysis of the normative force of such speech-acts as requests, promises and advice (Sciaraffa 2009, 255–259). My point, again, is simply about the inadequacy of Sciaraffa's account with respect to the concept of legal authority. In what follows a different account of content-independence is presented which suffers neither from the problems that afflict Hart's account nor from those that arise out of the association of content-independence with intention.

I propose, thus, that we understand a norm as providing a content-independent reason for action when the force of the norm derives from its source or status (the two being closely related, especially in the case of legal norms) and not from its soundness or wisdom.[3] (As I will explain shortly, this pertains not only to the intrinsic value of the norm, as it were, but also to the value of the effects of its application). It is important to emphasize not only what content-independence is associated with—namely, source and status—but also what it is contrasted with— namely, soundness or wisdom. Hart's talk of "nature or character" was too imprecise. The fact that a norm has a certain source is always, in a sense, part of its nature or character; but the fact that it has a certain source does not necessarily make it more or less sound (even if the likelihood of it being more or less sound is thereby enhanced). The sailor has a content-independent reason to swab the deck because *the captain issued a norm* to that effect, not because the captain's norm is wise. Legal norms provide content-independent reasons for action because they apply to subjects simply by virtue of being legal (a status which in turn depends on their having officially recognized sources) and not because they are wise in a moral, political or prudential sense. Thus, content-independent reasons might also be described as wisdom-independent; in fact, the latter phrase seems to capture the idea I want to convey more accurately than the former phrase does.

There is one more thing that can be said in order to clarify the notion of content-independence. Take the case of precedent. A judge can regard a prior judicial decision as normatively relevant in so far as it creates justified expectations relied upon by legal subjects, in particular the parties immediately before the judge. It should be clear that that judge is not taking the norm issued by the prior judicial decision as a content-independent reason for action; for the relevant reason does not depend on the mere fact *that the precedent norm makes a certain requirement*, but rather on the more complex fact *that the precedent norm's requirement creates a justified expectation*. The latter, more complex reason is not content-independent because it pertains to the "wisdom of the norm"—broadly construed to include not

---

[3] I might also have used the terms "reasonableness" or "correctness".

only the intrinsic value of the norm (e.g. the fact that it is just) but also the value of complying with it given the impact that it has had on the lives of others.[4]

Let us consider now what Hart deemed the other essential feature of authority, namely, peremptoriness. For Hart, an authoritative norm is supposed to cut off any independent deliberation on the merits pro and con of the prescribed action. Many scholars have argued that this account of peremptoriness is too strong, as it appears that a norm's authoritativeness does not depend on its ability to cut off *any* independent *deliberation* in respect of the soundness of the norm. There are two ways in which the requirement that a norm provide peremptory reasons may need to be relaxed. The first one was suggested by Raz: "I do all that the law requires of me if my actions comply with it. There is nothing wrong with my considering the merits of the law or of action in accord with it. Reflection on the merits of actions required by authority is not automatically prohibited by any authoritative directive...." (1985a, 7) Raz's point is that an authoritative norm is supposed to prevent subjects from letting their actions be guided by considerations about the merits of the norm, not that it necessarily prevents subjects from even thinking about the desirability of the actions that they obediently perform.[5]

Now, even Raz's somewhat weaker understanding of peremptoriness has been a target of intense criticism (Perry 1989; Alexander 1990; Waluchow 1994, 129–140). For Raz, the authoritativeness of a norm depends on its capacity to supply, not only a first-order reason for action in accord with the norm, but also a second-order reason to refrain from acting on (at least some) first-order reasons that pertain to the soundness of the action commanded by the norm. Critics regard this account as arbitrary and overly restrictive. There is nothing, they believe, that clearly impedes us from classifying as authoritative those norms that, while failing to *exclude* otherwise relevant first-order reasons, provide particularly weighty first-order reasons or perhaps (not to diverge too sharply from Raz's account) second-order reasons that significantly diminish the weight or prominence that some first-order reasons would otherwise have in our deliberations. So, for instance, even if

---

[4] The account of content-independence offered here finds inspiration in what Schauer (2009, Chap. 4) has recently said about the subject. I do not unqualifiedly endorse Schauer's views, however, because at times he seems to conflate the notions of content-independence and peremptoriness (or something like it): "[The force of rules and precedents] derives not from their soundness but from their status, and philosophers of law refer to this feature of authority as *content-independence*. When a rule (or a command, an order, or an instruction) is authoritative, its subjects are expected to obey regardless of their own opinions of its wisdom". (ibid., 62, footnote omitted). For me, a reason is content-independent if it applies to an agent simply by virtue of the fact that it can be associated with a certain source. The fact that a reason applies to an agent does not entail, however, that it preempts (or even overrides) all other possibly conflicting reasons. The peremptory nature of a reason is not to be confused with its content-independence, even though both features are possessed by authoritative reasons. Schauer's conflation is displayed in his assertion that a content-independent reason compels a subject to *obey* (a notion implying the existence of a conclusive reason to comply).

[5] But see Shapiro (2002, 406–407) for a claim to the effect that Hart never really held such a strong view of peremptoriness and therefore would not have disagreed with Raz.

the captain's command does not entirely prevent the sailor from acting on the consideration that fresh water is scarce and should not be wasted on a section of the ship that has recently been sanitized, the command can still be deemed authoritative as long as it diminishes the weight that this sort of consideration would normally have on the sailor's practical deliberation. Perhaps only when the scarcity of water achieves hazardous levels will the sailor be justified in disobeying the captain's command. It is not sufficient that the command provide an ordinary first-order reason for action that is not particularly weighty and also fails to alter the weight of possibly conflicting reasons (this insufficient, but necessary, condition of authority is covered by the requirement discussed earlier that an authoritative norm must be able to provide a content-independent reason for action). It also needs to be the case that the existence of the command makes it significantly harder than normal for conflicting reasons to carry the day. How much harder? It is difficult, perhaps impossible, to give a precise answer to this general question. All that Raz's critics are prepared to say is that an authoritative norm is not easily defeated by considerations having to do with the soundness of the prescribed action.

I have sympathy for Leiter's opinion that debates like the one between Raz and his critics amount to no more than a battle of conceptual intuitions, that is, intuitions about the correct application of the elusive concept of authority (Leiter 2007, 130–135). Unfortunately, battles of intuitions are distinctively short on argument and therefore philosophically unsatisfying. My own intuitions tend to align with those of Raz's critics but obviously this is not sufficient reason for rejecting Raz's account of authority. I am happy to announce however that for the purposes of this book, little rests on the adjudication of this dispute. I commit myself to the ecumenical view that authoritative reasons are content-independent and that they are ordinarily capable of defeating first-order reasons that bear on the wisdom or soundness of the relevant actions. I remain agnostic about whether authoritative reasons are second-order reasons that exclude first-order reasons, second-order reasons that diminish the weight of otherwise countervailing first-order reasons, or simply very weighty first-order reasons. It will become clear as we go along that these fine differences do not significantly affect my account of sources of law.

So what exactly does all this have to do with sources of law? Norms deriving from sources of law invariably provide content-independent reasons for action. Norms deriving from certain sources (in particular, the standard sources of legislation, precedent, and custom) are genuinely authoritative in the sense that they provide reasons that are not only content-independent but that also ordinarily defeat conflicting reasons that bear on the wisdom or soundness of the relevant action. Other sources of law (and this is a role that scholarship often plays in contemporary legal systems) produce norms that can be associated only with content-independent reasons for action. Such norms are not authoritative, as the reasons they provide are neither second-order reasons (exclusionary or otherwise) nor very weighty first-order reasons that ordinarily obligate agents to act in a certain way regardless of their warranted reservations about the wisdom of so doing. This is admittedly abstract and terse; more details about the relationship between sources of law and reasons for action will be provided in the next section.

On a final note, although I am trying to rely on an ecumenical account of authority, my analysis may still vex Razians insofar as it accepts as sources *of legal norms* sources of norms that are not authoritative but generate ordinary content-independent reasons for action. This does not indicate a disagreement with Raz's notion of authority, but it does indicate a disagreement with the Razian view that legal reasons are necessarily authoritative. I suspect, however, that my disagreement with Razians here would be largely verbal. By calling some non-authoritative norms "law" I do not assign to them an additional property over and above their content-independent-reason-giving nature. Nor do I use "law" as an honorific term. The notion of a source of law that does not generate authoritative norms—or, as I will describe it in the next section, the notion of a "permissive" source of law—should be used because of its usefulness for and currency among legal theorists, comparative lawyers, and legal professionals generally. I cannot show that Razians are utterly wrong in their restrictive use of the concept of law; but it is clear that they would, without good reason, alienate themselves if they were to deny the possibility of permissive sources of law.

3.2 Two Kinds of Sources of Law

Sources of law, in Hart's own terminology (1961, 247), can be either mandatory or permissive. Mandatory sources are those that judges are required to use and that generate norms that judges are (in most circumstances) required to follow. The use of permissive sources, on the other hand, is not required of judges; and the norms they provide are not especially weighty. What I understand as a permissive source is sometimes described by other authors as a "persuasive" source. There is good reason to prefer the term "permissive". Although not every source of law, as was indicated in the last section, can be associated with authoritative norms, I take it to be a necessary feature of a source of law that it be capable of issuing norms that function as content-independent reasons for action. You will recall that a content-independent reason for action is one whose existence is independent of the soundness or wisdom of the action that it recommends. An agent who acts on a content-independent reason does so regardless of whether or not he is *persuaded* that he has chosen the substantively correct course of action. This is a key feature of my account of sources of law and it should not be obscured by the use of the phrase "persuasive source".

Now, it should be acknowledged that the use of "persuasive source" is not entirely unmotivated. Since permissive sources do not issue authoritative norms, the content-independent reasons supplied by such sources are relatively more easily defeated by conflicting first-order reasons that bear on the soundness of the relevant actions. So if one is not persuaded that the action recommended by a norm deriving from a permissive source is wise, he can relatively casually refuse to enforce it. Indeed, he can even omit reference to the permissive source, as its use by definition is not required. As Bronaugh has said in the context of distinguishing between binding and persuasive precedent, judges may enforce binding precedent while expressing regret for having to do so. But no judge would regretfully enforce a persuasive precedent (Bronaugh 1987, 222–223). I accept Bronaugh's point in slightly modified form. A judge cannot—or, more precisely, *will not*—regretfully enforce a norm deriving from a permissive source because, presumably, his regret would arise out of the belief that the norm prescribes an unwise course of action. While an agent is ordinarily compelled to abide by an authoritative norm that leads to bad results, he is not compelled to abide by apparently unsound norms originating from permissive sources.

Let me recapitulate. Norms generated by permissive sources function as content-independent reasons for action. It is to avoid obscuring this fact that one should not describe them as persuasive sources. However, it is true that norms deriving from permissive sources, unlike mandatory norms, are not genuinely authoritative.[6] If one is not required to use permissive sources, then it is to be expected that one is not required to *enforce* the norms generated by them if they, the norms, strike one as being unsound. The worry might arise at this point that if a permissive source of law may be casually disregarded on the basis of substantive considerations, then it plays no significant role in the deliberations of officials. This is what P. K. Tripathi had to say in discussing the relevance of foreign precedent (a common example of a permissive source) to constitutional decision-making:

> When a judge looks to foreign legal systems for analogies that shed light on any of the new cases before him, he is looking to legal material which he is absolutely free to reject unless it appeals to his reason. Appeal to one's reason, more often than not, amounts to a confirmation and a strengthening of one's own opinion rather than a shaping of that opinion (As cited in McCrudden 2000, 516).

Tripathi believed that the irrelevance of foreign precedent is established when to these considerations it is added that in the majority of cases a judge can easily find foreign precedents that are inconsistent with the ones which appeal to his reason. The judge picks cherries: foreign precedents are no more than rationalizations of choices made on other, subjective grounds. This admittedly amounts to a strong case against the relevance of foreign precedent (although plausible responses to it are not hard to envisage: see McCrudden 2000, 517–527). But its strength depends on the peculiar fact that a judge has conflicting sources at his disposal. While this is a plausible contention in respect of foreign precedent (since foreign courts are so numerous and their opinions so diverse), it is unlikely to hold true of permissive sources generally. On the other hand, a fact described in the passage quoted above—namely, that foreign precedents strengthen but do not shape judicial opinion—does in fact apply to permissive sources generally. But it also helps to establish my view. By strengthening a judge's opinion, a permissive

---

[6] Green (2009, 20) has provided a similar account of permissive sources of law: "Permissive sources get the force they have, not from their merits, but from the fact that they are actually recognised and applied as reasons for decision in the practice of the courts. But they are weak reasons whose weight is variable".

source makes a difference which is not negligible. The following contrast will help to illustrate the point.

The opinion of a judge in a co-ordinate court of law (another standard example of a permissive source) is normally not accorded the same status as the opinion of, say, a noted newspaper editor. A judge typically only lets himself be guided (usually tacitly) by the editor's opinion if he finds it persuasive; he has no other reason to follow the editor's opinion in the justification of his decision. But the judge often does believe that part of the appeal of the opinion of a co-ordinate court is precisely that it is the opinion of that court. If the judge chooses to use the opinion (and admittedly he has the ability to choose whether or not to use it), he will cite to that ruling and will, along with his peers, regard this citation as providing additional support for his decision. This is the point that I have been trying to make by associating permissive sources with content-independent reasons for action. Stressing the defeasibility of such reasons does not undermine the importance of permissive sources: the defeasibility of a reason is not proof of its irrelevance.

The relevance of permissive sources is further shown by the fact that some sources are regarded as prohibited in certain jurisdictions. For instance, reference to decisions of foreign courts is prohibited, or at least regarded with suspicion, in some jurisdictions (even though it is permitted and even strongly encouraged in others: see McCrudden 2000, 511). So, a significant contrast exists not only between permissive sources of law and non-legal sources that are not usually cited and whose relevance depends entirely on their persuasiveness (e.g. the newspaper editor's opinion), but there is also a contrast to be heeded between permissive sources and sources whose use is to be avoided.

Now, there is no reason to believe that the important distinction between mandatory and permissive sources of law is a sharp distinction such that all instances of sources of law fall neatly onto one side or another of the divide. Commonly, in Schauer's words, "the status of an authority *as* an authority is the product of an informal and evolving process by which some sources become progressively more authoritative as they are increasingly used and accepted." (2009, 80) Or as Peczenik has suggested, between "must-sources" and "may-sources" one can also find "should-sources" (2005, 16). A "should-source" presumably is one that cannot casually be ignored (a brief or decision that ignored it would be subject to criticism even if not on the whole unsuccessful). And once used, a "should-source" probably provides a content-independent reason which, although not very weighty, is not as easily defeated by conflicting substantive considerations as are the reasons associated with "may-sources". This is to say that the distinction between mandatory and permissive sources of law should not be regarded as a sharp dichotomy. Relatedly, a source's status in a given jurisdiction tends to be somewhat fluid and subject to change.[7]

---

[7] Peczenik's terminology is useful, but it can also be misleading. In fact, to be perfectly honest, so can the use of the term "permissive": "We need to be cautious here, for if they are permissive

I have said that a mandatory source must always be used and should in most circumstances be enforced (or, more precisely, that the *norm* issued by the mandatory source should in most circumstances be enforced). Why do I deny that the relevant norm must always be enforced (while I accept that its source must always be *used*, i.e. referred to and dealt with)? Take the example of legislation, the paradigm instance of a mandatory source of law. Legislated norms are fully authoritative in most legal systems. This means that judges see themselves as normally bound to apply such norms regardless of the desirability of the results they prescribe. But most legal systems contain (largely tacit) secondary norms that allow for the departure from legislated norms in extreme cases, that is, when the result commanded by the legislated norm is too unreasonable to be tolerated.[8] As I will explain later, judges sometimes avoid the implications of legislated norms by affirming, in a way that may mitigate the defiant nature of their acts, that they refuse to apply the *plain or literal meaning* of a statute only to ensure that the true purpose (the principle or policy) behind the statute is enforced. At other times, when it cannot plausibly be argued that the purpose that underlies the statute is in conflict with its plain meaning, judges appeal to principles or policies whose relation to positive law is more remote. A plausible reading of *Riggs v. Palmer* attributes precisely that approach to the majority, who refused to apply the literal meaning of the applicable statute because it violated the unwritten principle that *no man may profit from his own wrong* (see Schauer 2004, 1937–1938).[9]

The same point applies to precedent where it is regarded as a mandatory source of law, i.e. where it is regarded as binding (Summers and Eng 1997, 524–526; Eisenberg 2007, 86–87). To be precise, the point applies more clearly in the case of horizontal precedent (where a court is bound by its own past decision) than it

---

(Footnote 7 continued)

sources, then they are not, as one might think, mere permissions, for sources are prima facie reasons for courts (and others) to *act*. But being permitted to φ is not normally any sort of reason to φ (though it may be a reason for others not to interfere with one's φ-ing)." (Green 2009, 19) Leslie Green does not distinguish between sources and norms like I do but he makes a good point that needs to be acknowledged. Lack of reference to permissive sources does not generate criticism and that is why we can say that they "may" be used. But this should not obscure the fact that the norms deriving from permissive sources have some weight; they are not norms that merely permit some act, but norms that effectively prescribe it (for further clarification, see the distinction between use and enforcement in the text below).

[8] This view finds support in the comparative studies collected in MacCormick and Summers (1991), which examine the practices of statutory interpretation of the highest courts of appeal or review in nine different jurisdictions. My remarks about *Riggs* in Chap. 2 point in the same direction.

[9] Considerations of policy and principle will have more power, and hence will more likely be used by judges defying mandatory sources, when it can plausibly be argued that the considerations in question have significant social support, that is, when they do not derive exclusively from the personal convictions of the judges but reflect aspirations of the wider community. See Eisenberg (1988, Chap. 4) for an argument to the effect that common law judges typically appeal to those considerations of policy and principle which they believe to have significant social support.

does in the case of vertical precedent (where a court is bound by the decision of a higher court). In the latter case, a judge's ability to depart from precedent (or, more precisely, from the norm derived from the precedent case) on substantive grounds tends to be much more limited; if a judge wants explicitly to avoid the effect of a precedent from a higher court he would be wise to distinguish it (Summers and Eng 1997, 524).

So, even norms deriving from mandatory sources can be defeasible. Their authoritative nature makes it so that the conditions for their defeat are not easily or routinely satisfied; but the conditions exist none the less. It is noteworthy that, once the relevant threshold is met, the degree of authoritativeness of mandatory norms may vary from one jurisdiction to the other, as scholars comparing judicial practice in England and the United Stated have pointed out before (Atiyah and Summers 1987). But mandatory norms everywhere significantly limit a judge's ability to appeal to substantive considerations of principle and policy. When using legislation or binding precedent judges will often have the experience that Bronaugh described as having regretfully to apply the law.

In explaining how a norm deriving from a mandatory source can be defeated I have employed an important distinction that is not usually explicitly made by legal theorists. The distinction is one between the notion of *using a source* and the notion of *enforcing the norm it generates*. Notice, accordingly, that the "must" in "must-source" refers to the use of the source, not necessarily to the enforcement of the norm, which is more accurately associated with a very strong (yet defeasible) "should". (How strong? That is hard to say: strong enough to justify talk of authoritativeness). So, a mandatory source is one which must be used (referred to, dealt with) and which issues norms that should (except in extreme circumstances) be applied.

A permissive source, on the other hand, is one that judges are not required to use (they *may* use the "may-source") but which, if used, issues a comparatively weak "should", that is, a content-independent but not fully authoritative "should". And, for the sake of completeness, a "should-source" should be used *and* should have its norm enforced in a sense of "should" that is fairly strong but not strong enough to count as authoritative.

A number of questions might arise at this point. Could there be, for instance, "must-sources" that generate norms that should only be applied in a weaker sense of "should"? In other words, could there be such a thing as a mandatory source that generates non-authoritative reasons for action? And, on the other hand, could there be permissive sources that, once used, generate authoritative reasons for action? These questions are perfectly sensible, for once the notion of use of a source and the notion of enforcement of the norm it issues are conceptually severed, combinations could arise other than the ones that characterize mandatory and permissive sources as I understand them. All that can really be said about this is that, although alternative combinations are conceivable, in practice they are probably very rare. For what would be the point of *demanding* reference to a source of norms that could casually be defeated? And why would judges be given *the option* of using a source which, once brought into a decision, would yield reasons which they would have a very hard time defeating?

References

Alexander L (1990) Law and exclusionary reasons. Philos Topics 18:5

Atiyah P, Summers R (1987) Form and substance in Anglo-American law. Clarendon Press, Oxford

Bronaugh R (1987) Persuasive precedent. In: Goldstein L (ed) Precedent in law. Clarendon Press, New York

Eisenberg M (1988) The nature of the common law. Harvard University Press, Cambridge

Eisenberg M (2007) The principles of legal reasoning in the common law. In: Edlin D (ed) Common law theory. Cambridge University Press, New York

Gardner J (2007) Some types of law. In: Edlin D (ed) Common law theory. Cambridge University Press, New York

Green L (2009) Law and the causes of judicial decisions. Oxford legal research paper series. Paper No. 14/2009. Available at http://ssrn.com/abstract=1374608. Accessed on 20 November 2011

Hart HLA (1961) The concept of law. Clarendon Press, Oxford

Hart HLA (1982) Commands and authoritative reasons. In: Hart HLA (ed) Essays on Bentham: jurisprudence and political theory. Oxford University Press, New York

Leiter B (2007) Naturalizing jurisprudence: essays on American legal realism and naturalism in legal philosophy. Oxford University Press, New York

MacCormick N, Summers R (eds) (1991) Interpreting statutes: a comparative study. Dartmouth, Aldershot

Markwick P (2003) Independent of content. Legal Theor 9:43

McCrudden C (2000) A common law of human rights? Transnational judicial conversations on constitutional rights. Oxford J Legal Stud 20:499

Peczenik A (2005) Scientia juria: legal doctrine as knowledge of law and as a source of law. Springer, Dordrecht

Perry S (1989) Second-order reasons, uncertainty and legal theory. South Calif Law Rev 62:913

Raz J (1985a) Authority and justification. Philos Public Aff 14:3

Raz J (1985b) Authority, law and morality. Monist 68:295

Schauer F (2004) The limited domain of law. Va Law Rev 90:1909

Schauer F (2009) Thinking like a lawyer. A new introduction to legal reasoning. Harvard University Press, Cambridge

Sciaraffa S (2009) On content-independent reasons: it's not in the name. Law Philos 28:233

Shapiro S (2002) Authority. In: Coleman J, Shapiro S (eds) The Oxford handbook of jurisprudence and philosophy of law. Oxford University Press, New York

Summers RS, Eng S (1997) Departures from precedent. In: MacCormick N, Summers RS (eds) Interpreting precedents: a comparative study. Dartmouth, Aldershot

Waluchow W (1994) Inclusive legal positivism. Oxford University Press, New York

Chapter 4
Legal Scholarship as a Source of Law

4.1 Standard Legal Scholarship

There are many kinds of academic writings that fall under the category of legal scholarship. On the broadest meaning of the term, any intellectual enterprise that takes law as its central subject matter would count as an exercise in legal scholarship. Why must law be the *central* subject matter? For we would arguably stretch the meaning of "legal scholarship" too far if we were to use it to describe works in which references to law were incidental or served exclusively as means for the achievement of other purposes. I recently read the biography of a Brazilian playwright, Nelson Rodrigues, whose controversial work (focusing on themes like adultery, prostitution, and crimes of passion) was often the object of official censorship. The biographer would sometimes have to explain a bit of the Brazilian law operating at the time in order to explain the reasons for the playwright's troubles. Important as these legal bits of the biography might have been, it would seem odd to describe the work as an instance of legal scholarship. I have no qualms about describing it as a piece of scholarship more generally, given the amount and depth of historical research behind it; but its references to the law were secondary in relation to the biographer's purpose of describing Rodrigues's life.

Now, the notion of "centrality" employed here is admittedly vague. There are cases in which it will be hard to determine whether a piece of scholarship qualifies as legal scholarship or not. To insist on the topic of biographies, Lacey's intellectual biography of Hart (2006) is not as easy to classify as the aforementioned biography of Rodrigues. In so far as the former book describes Hart's personal and professional life there is nothing "legal" about it. But the book also analyses Hart's jurisprudence quite extensively. Lacey's discussion of Hart's theory of law and methodology is not detached or merely expository but includes fairly bold and potentially controversial claims. Other jurists have found these claims relevant enough to merit detailed consideration (Farrell 2006). So, how central to Lacey's project was her analysis of Hart's legal theory? It is hard to say. Although I would intuitively classify her book as a piece of legal scholarship, it would be silly to quibble with someone who had a different intuition.

F. P. Shecaira, *Legal Scholarship as a Source of Law*,
SpringerBriefs in Law, DOI: 10.1007/978-3-319-00428-0_4,
© The Author(s) 2013

In any case, the broad concept of legal scholarship that I am introducing, although fuzzy at the edges, has clear and undisputed instances and non-instances. There is no point in discussing its non-instances but a word should be said about its instances. Philosophy of law, law and economics, law and literature, critical legal theory, sociology of law, legal history, legal anthropology, comparative law, inquiries into international law, and inquiries into the laws of any national juris-diction are perhaps the most common examples of legal scholarship in the broad sense. They are examples of intellectual undertakings that have law as their central subject matter. They vary significantly in approach and method, and they treat their common subject matter at different levels of abstraction; but they are all centrally concerned with law in one way or another, that is, with particular laws, or particular legal systems, or laws and legal systems as general categories, or even *the* law as an abstract entity.

A truly general account of legal scholarship would have to say something substantive about all these very different intellectual enterprises that have law as their central subject matter. I, however, am interested in discussing legal schol-arship *as a source of law*. In view of this, I will focus hereafter on one particular kind of legal scholarship. It is the sort of legal scholarship that is most likely to serve the function of a source of law in modern municipal legal systems, i.e. the sort of legal scholarship that judges in such systems are most likely to treat as providing norms that function as (more or less weighty) content-independent reasons for deciding cases in a particular way. I will be focusing on a sort of legal scholarship that is often described by legal scholars as "standard" (or "conven-tional" or "traditional" or "normal").

In the US, where literature about legal scholarship is particularly recent and rich, there is significant agreement about the broad characteristics of the sort of legal scholarship that counts as "standard" (see e.g., Dan-Cohen 1992; Friedman 1998; Gordon 1993; Posner 2002; Rakoff 2002; Rhode 2002; Rubin 1988, 1992; Saks et al. 1994; Schauer 1991; Schlag 1992; Tushnet 1987). As much and as deeply as American scholars may disagree about the merits of standard legal scholarship, about whether to be pessimistic or optimistic about its future, and about how to improve it where improvement is needed, they seem to agree sig-nificantly about what standard legal scholarship is.

So what is standard legal scholarship? It can be identified by reference to three related characteristics: (1) it is prescriptive; (2) it is directed not only at other scholars but also at legal officials and practitioners; and (3) it employs a discourse and style of argument that is typical of the legal professionals who form part of its audience. These features will be explained in turn.

First, to say that standard legal scholarship is prescriptive is not to say that it necessarily formulates its theses in terms of "oughts" (scholars, like judges, often prefer to present their views in terms of what the law "is" or "requires") but rather that it is capable of *providing* (as opposed to simply reporting officially sanctioned) solutions to *fairly specific* legal questions. At this early point one might already wonder, "Is there not a common type of legal scholarship that is exclusively critical of, say, a judicial decision or a piece of legislation? In what sense would this kind of scholarship, which appears to be standard in an intuitive sense, perform the constructive task of *providing a solution* to a legal question?" But standard scholarship is rarely exclusively critical, and the reason why this is so will only become fully clear once the other features of standard scholarship are explained. To anticipate some of what will come shortly, standard scholarship does not freely employ extra-legal arguments; it argues fundamentally on the basis of legal doctrine, that is, on the basis of rules established in traditional sources of law, such as precedent, legislation and custom. That being the case, a scholar that is critical of, say, a judicial decision cannot simply attack it on moral grounds and still hope to have his work recognized as a piece of standard legal scholarship. That scholar must attempt to show, even if moral argument is an important part of his case, that the judicial decision is wrong or objectionable *as a matter of law*. This sort of criticism, and here is my point, is rarely articulated without the proposal of a particular interpretation of the conventional sources. In other words, it is rarely articulated without the proposal of an answer to the legal question at issue, an answer to be contrasted with that which was provided in the relevant decision. Indeed, even if the scholar does not appear to intend his work to be at all constructive (that is, if he explicitly does nothing but criticize), it is still not unlikely that from his examination of the legal basis of the judicial decision practical implications can readily be drawn. In a sense, scholarship from which practical implications are easily drawn is prescriptive, even if not deliberately or explicitly so.

It should also be noted that the presence of highly abstract theoretical contentions does not render a piece of legal scholarship non-standard provided that its author draws out (or that his reader be readily able to do draw out) the implications of his abstract claims in an attempt to provide a solution to a more concrete legal problem. For instance, an argument for a particular interpretation of a particular constitutional provision might very well begin with lofty claims about the nature and function of constitutions. Practical accounts of tort law may begin with philosophical discussions of the relations between corrective justice, distributive justice and economic efficiency. Juristic discussion of criminal punishment may hinge on philosophical theories of just desert and social utility. And so on.

The importance of the prescriptive nature of legal scholarship—i.e. its ability to provide solutions to fairly specific legal questions—in relation to its capacity to function as a source of law is illustrated in an interesting study by Farber (2000). Farber compares the decisions of two jurisprudentially minded American judges sitting on the same court: Frank Easterbrook and Richard Posner. According to Farber, "[i]n terms of their theoretical writings about interpretation, Posner (a leading pragmatist) and Easterbrook (a leading textualist) are as far apart as two judges could be" (ibid. 1409). Surprisingly, however, in deciding particular legal questions, Easterbrook sometimes comes out sounding pragmatic while Posner sticks to the legal text. Farber's point is not, by any means, that Easterbrook and Posner are careless or incapable of consistently applying their abstract interpretive theories. In fact, a careful examination of the judges' arguments shows that their judgments are entirely consistent with their broader jurisprudential views. Farber's point, or at least the claim which I think he is capable of substantiating, is rather that an awareness of Easterbrook's and Posner's jurisprudence does not permit one easily to predict how exactly the two judges are going to deal with particular cases. That being the case, the judges' jurisprudential works would not serve as great guides for action: a third judge would probably find it difficult to use Easterbrook's or Posner's general writings on interpretive methodology while attempting to solve particular legal disputes. What renders a piece of scholarship prescriptive (as I am using the term) is its practical nature and ability to give guidance with respect to fairly specific legal issues.[1]

The claim that standard legal scholarship is directed at legal officials also needs to be appropriately qualified. Dan-Cohen (1992, 589–592) has suggested that the relationship between authors of prescriptive legal scholarship and judges is akin to the relationship between actors in a play and individuals who come to watch. Actors do not engage spectators in dialogue, and scholars, similarly, do not have

---

[1] It should be emphasized that highly theoretical writings are not ignored by courts if they are ultimately prescriptive, or if, in spite of their abstractness, they have clear implications with respect to particular cases. The fact that highly theoretical scholarship is not entirely ignored by judges is shown by an interesting study regarding the citation practices of American courts: "... many of the articles frequently cited by courts are highly theoretical. In addition to the economic analyses noted above, William Eskridge and Philip Frickey draw upon Aristotle's theory of practical reasoning to propose a theory of statutory interpretation; Cass Sunstein includes extensive theoretical discussion of the proper relationship between law and administration in his highly cited article about statutory interpretation after Chevron; Kathleen Sullivan invokes a variety of philosophical and economic theories to critique unconstitutional conditions; Richard Fallon and Daniel Meltzer summon jurisprudential theory to analyze the problem of retroactivity across a broad spectrum of constitutional cases; and Akhil Amar proposes unifying theories for treating the Bill of Rights as a whole. These and other articles on our lists demonstrate that courts do not eschew theoretical discussions by scholars, as long as they perceive those discussions as helpful in resolving the controversies before them" (Merritt and Putnam 1996, 888, footnotes omitted). The willingness of American courts to entertain abstract theory on occasion is not exceptional: Markesinis, discussing the decisions of the German Federal Court, claims that their arguments can be "highly conceptual, even metaphysical" (1986, 352), although their conclusions must inevitably be very concrete. One should, of course, keep an eye out for references to abstract scholarship that are presented *as if* they were capable of offering significant guidance to judges when in fact they are not. As I will explain in Chap. 6, judges can use legal scholarship in misleading ways. One such way involves suggesting that a scholar's opinion guides a judge's decision when in fact that opinion is too vague to make an important practical difference. I am suspicious, to give just one example, of the references that the Supreme Court of Canada has made to Elmer Driedger's claim that "[t]oday there is only one principle or approach [to statutory interpretation], namely, the words of an Act are to be read in their entire context and in their grammatical and ordinary sense harmoniously with the scheme of the Act, the object of the Act, and the intention of Parliament." (cited, e.g., in *R v Ulybel Enterprises Ltd.*, [2001] 2 S.C.R. 867, para 28). There is a lot of room for reasonable disagreement about what the "scheme" and "object" of an Act are, and about how one is to go about determining the intention of Parliament. But no mention of the possibility of disagreement is made in *R v Ulybel* and other decisions citing Driedger's famous passage, which apparently is treated as if its meaning were clear.

judges as their immediate interlocutors. Scholars, while producing scholarship, have other scholars as their interlocutors. A scholar writes up the draft of a paper and circulates it among his peers. After working on that paper for some time, the scholar submits it to a journal with the hope that the editors of the journal and its reviewers will react positively. Who are the editors and the reviewers of the journal? Other scholars, of course (or perhaps aspirant scholars, in the case of the typical American law review editor). If published, eventually the paper will reach a wider audience, which includes legal officials and practitioners. Dan-Cohen's point is that although the content of the legal scholar's work may have appeal for judges and lawyers, the fact that it would not have seen the light of day were it not for the assent of other scholars significantly shapes the author's approach. He needs to persuade his peers before he persuades judges or anyone else.

Fair enough. Dan-Cohen's point serves as a warning to those who might tend to overemphasize the importance of the fact that standard legal scholarship has officials and practitioners as part of its intended audience. Excessive emphasis on this point would obscure the fact that standard legal scholarship is, because of the nature of the review process through which it goes prior to publication, quite scholarly. But, of course, we should also not commit the opposite mistake of downplaying the importance of the fact that officials and practitioners are among the expected readership of standard legal scholarship. This is one of the things that make this kind of legal scholarship distinctive. Knowing that they are dealing with the same issues which officials and practitioners encounter in their professional lives, and expecting that at least some of these officials and practitioners will be curious enough to read scholarly work, scholars construct their arguments accordingly.

This leads us to the third feature of standard legal scholarship, namely, that it uses a discourse and style of argument that are quite similar to those used by judges and legal practitioners. Judges tend to base their arguments on conventional sources. If there is an applicable statute or precedent whose plain meaning provides a clear solution to the case at hand judges will normally apply the statute or precedent. Judges will only resort to overtly substantive arguments (i.e. moral, political or economic arguments) when there is no clear rule of positive law disposing of the case, or when the rule is clear enough but provides a solution which is exceedingly unsatisfactory (from a moral, political or economic point of view). And even in these circumstances—namely, when the applicable rule is unclear or dictates a very unsatisfactory result—a judge's willingness to resort to substantive argument is fairly limited. Judges rarely refer to substantive principles or policies without attempting to show that such principles and policies are connected in important ways to the very rules which they, the judges, find themselves unable to apply. A principle or policy is typically presented as the true, underlying purpose of a rule of positive law, or sometimes as the rationale which unifies an entire body of such rules.

One helpful way to describe these features of judicial discourse is to say that it is formalist[2] (more will be said about this notion in the next chapter, and about the different, although importantly related, senses in which it is used). A discourse is formalist when it acknowledges obstacles to the use of arguments or considerations which would be deemed perfectly appropriate outside of the bureaucratic environment in which the discourse is employed. Judges appeal first to rules previously laid down (in the form of legislation or precedent) or customarily enforced by other officials to whom they defer. Whether the rules issuing from these officials prescribe results that are wise from a substantive perspective is a question that is often put to the side (as the perceptive reader will have noticed, the formalist character of judicial discourse is closely related to the content-independence of the reasons provided by legal norms).[3]

Like judicial discourse, standard legal scholarship is significantly formalist. It is true that legal scholars have a thing for hard cases, and also that such cases usually require recourse to substantive arguments. Easy cases—i.e. cases settled without question by easily identifiable rules of positive law—tend to receive less scholarly attention than cases that are technically complicated and highly politically charged. Such cases, the hard ones, cannot be dealt with simply by reference to the plain meaning of the applicable statute or precedent; substantive arguments must be used. However, even in hard cases standard legal scholarship attempts to respect the limits to the use of substantive arguments that circumscribe the discourse of the legal profession—i.e. appropriate connections must be found between the relevant substantive considerations and the applicable legal rules. This is how Wendel has described the structure of this sort of argument:

> The argument proceeds like this: (1) Here is some legal doctrine or rule; (2) courts and scholars (or at least my rivals) tend to think that its point, rationale, purpose, or function is X – that is, the doctrine is "all about" X; (3) but I think they're mistaken, and the doctrine is really "all about" Y; (4) here is some evidence supporting my claim; (5) therefore, we should understand the point of this rule or doctrine as Y (Wendel 2011, 1035).

---

[2] Neil MacCormick (1993, 17–18) used the equally helpful adjective "institutional" (contrasting "institutional argumentation" with "pure practical argumentation").

[3] For the sake of completeness, there is another respect in which judicial discourse is formalist. In the text I focus on judicial reliance on rules regulating primary behavior. But it is also the case that judges let themselves be guided by procedural rules (prescribing forms of action, assigning burdens of argument and specifying admissible evidence) that contribute significantly to the bureaucratic feel of their discourse. This is illustrated quite well in a hypothetical legal argument imagined by Prakken and Sartor (2004, 129): "—Plaintiff: I claim that defendant owes me 500 euros.—Defendant: I dispute plaintiff's claim.—Judge: Plaintiff, prove your claim.—Plaintiff: Defendant owes me 500 euros since we concluded a valid sales contract, I delivered but defendant did not pay.—Defendant: I concede that plaintiff delivered and I did not pay, but I dispute that we have a valid contract.—Judge: Plaintiff, prove your claim that you have a valid contract.—Plaintiff: This document is an avidavit, signed by us.—Defendant: I dispute that this document is an avidavit.—Judge: Defendant, since the document looks like an avidavit, prove that it is not.—Defendant: This lab report shows that the notary's signature was forged.—Plaintiff: That evidence is inadmissible, since I received it too late.—Judge: I agree: The evidence is inadmissible".

And Wendel helpfully distinguishes between arguments that appeal to substantive considerations in this limited fashion and what he dubs "frankly normative arguments":

> A frankly normative argument is one that asserts that some desirable state of affairs will be brought about if the law is understood in a particular way, or possibly reformed along certain lines. Consider a hypothetical paper one might encounter, arguing that the separation between investment banks and commercial banks created by the Glass-Steagall Act of 1933 should be reimposed because doing so would mitigate conflicts of interest that potentially expose depositors to excessive risks. ...The most important distinction between frankly normative arguments and those considered here... is that [the latter], by [their] very nature, [concern themselves] with rhetorical practices that are internal to law, avoiding reliance on extralegal normative considerations (Ibid. 1039).

In sum, standard legal scholarship is prescriptive, formalist and directed at legal professionals. The following questions may be raised at this point: "Why is this kind of scholarship described as 'standard'? Is that intended as an evaluative judgment? Is so-called 'standard' legal scholarship supposed to serve as a model which other kinds of legal scholarship should emulate or as a criterion by reference to which their merits should be assessed?" The main reason for my focus on scholarship that is prescriptive, formalist and intended for professionals (I will use "formalist" in the remainder of this chapter as an abbreviated description of these three related features) is that it is the kind of scholarship that, given its subject matter, style and practical orientation, is most likely to serve the function of a source of law. Judges (i.e. those who have the power to constitute a piece of scholarship as a source of law) have a practical job to do and are subject to strict professional requirements: that is to say, judges must settle real legal disputes and must do so in accordance with constraints related to the ideal of the rule of law. Given this predicament, it is natural that, in searching for scholarly assistance, judges should resort to a type of work that is oriented towards practical questions and also argues for practical conclusions by reference to standards that judges themselves could use without being accused of deviating from the rule of law. Standard legal scholarship fits the description.

This would certainly be enough to warrant my concern with standard legal scholarship, but it might not be enough to justify my calling it "standard". To be clear, "standard" is not used here as an evaluative term; instead it implies statistical predominance, or (if the object described as standard is not predominant at a particular moment in time) that there is a tendency for it to be predominant, and that whatever factors are temporarily counteracting that tendency are unlikely to prevail in the long run. The non-evaluative use of the term "standard" captures what so many American scholars seem to have in mind: it is an issue of statistical predominance or tendency thereto. Indeed, the numbers in the US suggest that formalist scholarship prevails (Saks et al. 1994, 1181). Even those who put significant emphasis on recent transformations in American legal scholarship have admitted this fact. Posner, for instance, begins a recent article with the claim that "legal scholarship has undergone changes so fundamental as to suggest the need for a reassessment of law as an academic discipline, as a subject of study, and as an intellectual institution" (2002, 1314). But he soon qualifies that strong claim by saying that "[d]octrinal scholarship continues; indeed, it continues to dominate legal scholarship if one counts the number of articles, student notes, treatises, casebooks, and textbooks, and even more so if one weights the number of publications by number of pages" (ibid. 1317, footnote omitted). What Posner understands by doctrinal scholarship is similar to what I describe as formalist scholarship (ibid. 1314–1317). There is a difference in that, for Posner, doctrinal scholarship is not interdisciplinary. I do not place an equivalent restriction on my definition of formalist scholarship: abstract and extralegal arguments can be used in formalist scholarship as long as these arguments are effectively employed in the examination of fairly specific legal questions, and as long as the relevant connections are articulated between such arguments and considerations based on rules of positive law. Given that my definition is less restrictive than Posner's, the kind of scholarship on which I focus is likely to be even more pervasive in the US than doctrinal scholarship.[4]

A related reason that may motivate American scholars to treat formalist legal scholarship as standard has to do with their imagined profile of the typical legal scholar. I have not seen statistics backing up this assumption, but it is certainly not implausible that lawyers, law professors who have practiced law for some time, and professors who have at least been to law school compose the majority of the scholars who focus exclusively or predominantly on the study of the law. That being the case, and as long as we grant the further plausible assumptions that such scholars tend to be practically minded and that they are very interested in the activities of the courts and the legal profession more generally, it seems safe to conclude that the statistical predominance of formalist legal scholarship is grounded on fairly stable features of its authorship. Formalist scholarship currently prevails numerically and there is little reason to think that the factors behind this dominance are significantly subject to change (in the US and elsewhere). Jestaz (2001, 5–20) provides a history of French legal scholarship which describes significant transformations in the relationship between scholars and legal practice. For instance, the fall of the *Ancien Régime* and the gradual development of case law thereafter helped to put an end to centuries of alienation of scholarship relative to practice. So, while it must be admitted that there are factors that can affect the practical orientation of legal scholars, it must also be emphasized that these factors are related to structural political and social realities, i.e. realities that are not easily

---

[4] My conception of formalist scholarship is very similar to Rakoff's (2002, 1281) account of "embedded" scholarship: "… it is possible to have legal scholarship that richly considers cases, statutes, and the like—embedded legal scholarship—which is also theoretically rich and, still further, sophisticated in its use of the methods of other disciplines". For Rakoff, scholarship that "richly considers" cases, statutes and the like is scholarship where "the problems that the authoritative materials present are resolved, the reasoning of those materials is taken seriously, and the boundaries of the existing law, while not necessarily given obeisance, are delimited" (ibid. 1280).

created or changed. After all, it took nothing less than an absolute monarchy to keep French legal scholars away from legal practice.

So, there is a kind of scholarship that deserves to be treated as standard. To be clear, this is not an American peculiarity[5]; what is described here as standard legal scholarship will probably be recognized by civil law theorists as "legal dogmatics":

> Legal science involves many branches, for example, legal sociology, legal history, jurisprudence, comparative law, and so on. Its central part consists, however, of legal dogmatics ("*Rechtsdogmatik*") which one may also call doctrinal study of law, analytical-evaluative study of the substance of law, etc. Legal dogmatics consists in the interpretation and systematization of legal norms. It seems that legal dogmatics uses a method similar in principle to the judicial method, although legal scholars have no power to decide cases and they think in a more general manner than judges. Yet, legal dogmatics constructs various "theories", for example, about the purpose of punishment, the meanings of some concepts, the nature and function of various legal institutions (marriage, ownership, etc.), the systematic connections between various parts of a given branch of law, e.g., civil law, and others. In Europe, a theory of legal reasoning *must* recognize the importance of legal dogmatics (Peczenik 1985, 289, footnote omitted).

My comments so far have been exclusively about the content of legal scholarship. All legal scholarship is about law, of course, and different kinds of legal scholarship examine law from different angles (e.g. normative or descriptive, historic or economic) and at different levels of abstraction and generality. Now, in addition to differences pertaining to content, legal scholarship can also be sorted into different groups according to form of publication. Legal scholarship appears variously in the form of journal articles, encyclopedia entries, case notes, treatises, monographs, commentaries, etc.[6] These distinctions are important because, as I will explain more carefully in the next section, the form in which legal scholarship is published can affect the way it is treated by judges. Different jurisdictions privilege different forms of publication. In the US, for instance, journal articles have a prominence (measured by frequency of citation in judicial decisions) which they do not have in England (Kötz 1990, 188). Case notes are particularly big in France. Commentaries, which are not common everywhere, are cited frequently by German courts (ibid. 193).[7]

---

[5] See Ross (1959, 46–48, 109), Nino (1974, 5–6, 28–34), Ferraz Jr (1998, 9–14), Aarnio (2011, 19), and Guastini (2011) for non-American testimony to the effect that something very close to what I am describing as standard legal scholarship has a prominent position within legal research.

[6] These are some of the more traditional (and still prevailing) forms in which legal scholarship appears. As we witness transformations in academic writing that include the "emergence of the short form, the obsolescence of exclusive rights, and the trend toward... disintermediation" (Solum 2006, 1071), new forms of legal scholarship, such as blog posts, SSRN papers and Wikipedia entries, appear and gain importance.

[7] This is what a commentary consists in according to Kötz: "A 'commentary' of a given statute... follows the structure of the enactment by stating for each article or section the court decisions, legal writing, and other materials that are relevant to a proper interpretation of what the article or section says. Some commentaries will also discuss the cases and draw from them a body of coherent doctrine" (1990, 193, footnote 36).

"Standard" status pertains exclusively to the content of scholarship; there is no clear standard relating to form of publication that applies across jurisdictions. Given its privileged position as a candidate source of law, it is on standard legal scholarship that I will be focusing. Indeed, for the sake of brevity, from now on I will drop the adjective "standard". Any unqualified reference to legal scholarship should henceforth be understood as a reference to standard legal scholarship, i.e. prescriptive, formalist, judge-and-practitioner-oriented legal scholarship. The next section will focus on (standard) legal scholarship as a source of law.

A final note on terminology is in order. Terms such as "the doctrine" and "legal dogmatics" are frequently used in civil law jurisdictions. I have already suggested that legal dogmatics correspond to standard legal scholarship. The correspondence is important for the purpose of comparative legal analysis. If a civil law scholar were to make an assertion about the use of legal dogmatics in the courts of his jurisdiction, I could probably translate the claim in terms of the use of standard legal scholarship in that jurisdiction. Something might be lost in the translation, given that the terms appear to have different connotations; but the terms still refer essentially to the same thing, namely, formalist juristic writings. "The doctrine" is also translatable in terms of standard legal scholarship. In light of its etymology (Jestaz 2005, 116) the best translation of "the doctrine" would arguably be "an influential body of teachings (concerning the law)". To describe someone as contributing to the doctrine is therefore to put some emphasis on his role as a *teacher*, whereas "scholarship" is more readily associated with the role of *researcher*. My view, again, is that despite interesting differences pertaining to what the terms connote, they denote roughly the same thing. Nothing of importance is lost in the translation.

4.2 The Potential of Legal Scholarship

While some scholars downplay the importance of legal scholarship as a source of law, others paradoxically overestimate its importance. Let us begin by addressing the latter tendency, which is grounded on weaker arguments.

It is true that judges and practitioners do not learn about the law, especially when they first begin their training and are therefore most impressionable, just by reading cases and legislation. They learn about the law also, if not primarily, by reading works written by scholars (and by listening to professors) who attempt to summarize and impose order on the vast and somewhat unsystematic array of norms found in laws and judicial decisions. The fact that scholarship mediates the relation between judges and practitioners, on the one hand, and legal norms, on the other, may have led some to the conclusion that legal scholarship is one of the most influential sources of law. For, arguably, a very large part of what law-making officials produce reaches the judge and the practitioner only after passing through the interpretive sieve of the scholar; and, it may be further argued, the scholar does not simply retrieve and reproduce in more accessible terms what officials meant to enact, but rather shapes it, supplements it, and purges it of inconsistencies and substantive defects. In a word, a large part of what judges and practitioners work with has been reconstructed by scholarship after leaving the hands of officials: scholars are co-authors, not mere mouthpieces, of the law.

This picture of the active mediating role of scholarship probably contains a number of exaggerations. The most worrisome of these exaggerations consists in depicting statutes and precedents as lumps of clay which can easily be molded by the hands of creative sculptors, i.e. the legal scholars. But that is a misleading depiction of positive law. It assumes that it has a malleability which in fact it lacks. Statutes and precedents, as soon as they are made public, contain a relatively fixed core of clear meaning. They are expressed in language whose meaning can easily be understood and applied by their addressees. This is not to deny, of course, that statutes and precedents can be vague, ambiguous, incoherent or otherwise indeterminate; nor is it to deny that they sometimes prescribe such unsatisfactory courses of action that their addressees will feel compelled to deviate from them. The point is that indeterminacy and gross substantive inadequacy are not the norm but the exception.[8] This is true for everyone whom the law addresses, including scholars who might be tempted to reshape it. No matter how great the temptation, there is only so much a scholar can do without conspicuously distorting the law. The scholar is constrained by the law's determinacy and soundness (or at least acceptability) with respect to the ordinary case; his capacity to serve as a co-author is thus significantly limited. This is especially true in respect of the law school classroom, where the scholar's principal aim is to teach current law to beginners, not to produce novel arguments and otherwise push the boundaries of the discipline (this is the sort of thing a scholar will more often do in papers prepared for publication in scientific journals).

Another problem that afflicts the view under consideration is that it risks confusing the issue of scholarship's causal influence on legal practice with its role as a formal source of law, i.e. as a source issuing norms that judges regard themselves as being bound (or having reason) to apply. There is much, apart from the books that judges read in law school, which colors their view of law and life. But it is very difficult to identify the endless factors that influence a judge's outlook, and, in any case, from a Hartian perspective, they do not matter much if they fail to play a significant part in legal reasoning and argumentation.

I should now turn to the other extreme, namely, that of downplaying the importance of legal scholarship. There are at least two ways in which the importance of legal scholarship can be minimized. The first way consists in raising doubts about the very possibility that legal scholarship may serve as a source of law. The other way acknowledges the status of scholarship as a permissive source

---

[8] The point I am trying to make here can alternatively be expressed through the claim that the routine legal case is easy, not hard. Critical Legal Scholars (Crits) are often described as having provided the most significant challenge to this intuitive claim. Persuasive answers to the Crits' challenge are found in Kress (1989), Schauer (1985), and Solum (1988).

of law but downplays the importance of permissive sources generally. These two positions will be considered in turn.

Rubin (1992) argues that there is an important difference between the kind of authority that is sometimes accorded to legal scholarship and the kind of authority that is associated with other sources of law. The authority of a legislator is based on his hierarchical position while the authority of a scholar depends on the quality of his work. A scholar may aspire to play the role of a hierarchical authority but can never actually achieve that status:

> Scholars know, of course, that this is not realistic; they recognize that their effect on public decisionmakers must be based on the content of their work, and will be continuously open to challenge. "But perhaps," whispers that voice, "I can present my views in such a compelling manner that the decisionmakers I address will follow me as if I were a true, hierarchical authority." The mechanism by which such an effect would be achieved is persuasion. When a person is persuaded by another's argument, he adopts that argument as his own, while consciously recognizing its source. Thus, persuasion is the content-based equivalent of true authority (ibid. 748).

First, a terminological note is in order. I do not use the word "authority" quite like Rubin does. You will recall that, for me, a norm is fully authoritative if and only if it provides a content-independent reason for action which normally defeats conflicting substantive reasons not to act as the norm requires. Thus, I would have no problem with the claim that legal scholarship is not typically authoritative if that is understood to mean that legal scholarship typically provides content-independent reasons which are not especially weighty (although later I will take issue with the view that legal scholarship does not *ever* issue authoritative reasons). But when Rubin denies authoritative status to legal scholarship he also refuses to acknowledge that legal scholarship can realistically[9] be associated with content-independent reasons for action. For Rubin, legal scholarship's impact on legal decision-making is always dependent on its ability to persuade the decision-maker. *That a particular scholar said so* is never by itself a reason for action. What the scholar says must persuade in order for it to generate reasons for action.

To concede this point to Rubin would be to deny the possibility that legal scholarship may function as a genuine source of law. For I have defined a source of law as possessing the capacity to issue norms which function as content-independent reasons for action. *That a particular scholar said so* must be capable of generating a reason for action, whether what was said by the scholar strikes one as argumentatively compelling or not. Now, I do not want to deny that the authority of legal scholarship is usually in some way connected to the perceived quality of its content. But the connection is not always as direct as Rubin imagines. Consider what Schauer has to say about the issue:

---

[9] It is not clear whether Rubin is making a conceptual point or rather a point about the negligible likelihood that scholarship will function as an "authority" (in his sense). The arguments in this section should show that, on either interpretation, Rubin is mistaken.

> Although optional authorities are sometimes selected because they are persuasive, more often they are selected *as authorities* because the selector trusts the authority as an authority even if he does not agree with the conclusion, or more likely, believes himself unreliable in reaching a conclusion on which the authority, whether commentator or other court, is thought more reliable (2009, 71).
>
> We can now see that a common use of an optional authority is not one in which the judge is persuaded by the substance of what an optional source says, but instead is one in which she is persuaded that the source is more likely to be right than she would be if she made her own decision (ibid. 72).

Apart from some terminological differences, I agree with Schauer. Judges sometimes treat a piece of scholarship as providing reasons for action because it is the work of an author whose intellect is widely admired; or because it appeared in a journal recognized for the sophistication of the articles it publishes; or because the author is affiliated with a prestigious research institution. The relevance of the piece of scholarship is normally connected to the perception that its author or venue has consistently produced high quality work in the past. But the point that needs to be emphasized is that the source's praiseworthy performance in the past allows it to enjoy a status that shelters it somewhat from the kind of scrutiny that Rubin has in mind. A presumption is created in favor of the quality of the opinions of a noted source. A judge may not be convinced by the opinion of a noted commentator, he may not even understand the commentator's intricate reasoning, but he may still see it as providing a reason for action. *That that particular commentator said so* is in and of itself normatively relevant for the judge. It is certainly true that a scholar's status as a reliable source may be put into question if the quality of his work declines conspicuously or loses relevance with the passage of time. (That is what I mean by the fact that a scholar's status is only *somewhat* sheltered from critical scrutiny.) Thus, the claim made here is not that those using a scholar's work as a source of law entirely and indefinitely renounce looking into his reasoning and considering its soundness, but rather that they take the quality of the work for granted at least while there is no glaring reason to do otherwise.

Another way to make the argument is to point to the fact that considerations that go into the justification of the authority of a source, or of its capacity to generate content-independent reasons, do not play a part in the (content-independent) reasoning that follows the recognition of a source as authoritative or as capable of generating content-independent reasons. The quality of an author's work is often what grounds the assignment of the status of a source of law to what he produces. But once the status has been assigned (no formal act necessarily marks this occasion; it is often a slow, gradual process), the author's opinions are treated as having weight independently of their capacity to persuade. To show that—*pace* Rubin—there is no essential difference between hierarchical authority and the sort of authority that might be assigned to scholarly writings, we have only to consider that the kind of consideration that goes into the justification of the latter can also go into the justification of the former. The expertise of officials (e.g. employees of regulatory agencies, members of specialized committees in legislatures) can justify the ascription of authority to them. The fact that certain bodies (e.g. democratic legislatures, constitutional courts) use decision procedures that are likely to conduce to right answers to certain legal and moral problems can also help to justify their authority. No one would (or should) contend that such officials and institutions are any less authoritative just because the reasons behind their authoritativeness have to do with the quality of their reasoning or with the fact that their procedures are conducive to wise decisions. A good example is provided by the practice of according additional weight to the decisions of noted judges and to decisions delivered after reflection:

> The attention which later courts pay to a precedent will depend very much on how judges and lawyers assess it as an effort at legal reasoning.... In English law, law reporters can increase the likelihood that a decision will be treated as especially authoritative by signalling – through the insertion of *cur. adv. vult* after the arguments of counsel – that judgment was reserved (i.e., only delivered after some reflection) rather than delivered extempore at the conclusion of the case (Duxbury 2008, 65).

English judges, according to Duxbury, assign more weight to precedent which they regard as more likely to be grounded on good reasoning. A presumption that the reasoning behind a decision delivered after reflection is better than it would otherwise have been (had the decision been delivered *extempore*) is something that can render the precedent weightier. My point is that if there is no reason to doubt that the increased authoritativeness of a precedent can be based on the perception that it possesses a distinctive feature that makes it more likely to be based on sound reasoning, then there is no reason to doubt that scholarship's capacity to function as a source of content-independent reasons can be grounded on the perception that it is based on good reasoning.

The reader may find the foregoing account of the use of scholarship conceptually coherent and yet have doubts about its applicability in the analysis of real judicial decisions. Indeed, Flanders has expressed reservations in this regard:

> ... it is not clear that the trust in this [sort of] case is wholly divorced from the content of the reasoning. A court may pay special attention to a decision by [e.g.] Richard Posner, but it will not defer to him independently of what he says. It just means that the court has previously found Posner a good judge to turn to when facing a difficult problem (2009, footnote 53).[10]

Flanders's remark prompts some important observations. I insist that it is conceptually possible for a judge to treat a piece of scholarship as a genuine source of law while doing so for the reason that it is authored by an expert (as distinct from the reason that the author has presented a persuasive argument in that particular instance). But it must be conceded that it is also possible, as Flanders seems to suggest in mentioning Posner, for a judge to regard an author as an expert, to privilege his work over that of others, and yet only to regard that author's opinion as reason-giving when it is based on persuasive arguments. And I must concede further that it will not always be easy to determine in which of these two ways

---

[10] Flanders mentions only Posner's judicial decisions (as opposed to his academic works), but the point he makes can clearly be extended to scholarship.

(either as a genuine source of law or not) scholarship is being treated by judges who cite it. So why do I think that it can be done?

One important piece of evidence indicating that judges are using scholarship as a genuine source of law occurs when judges state the conclusion of a scholarly work while making summary reference, if any, to the argument which grounds it. Indeed, judges very often provide bibliographical references and produce a brief quotation without giving any suggestion that its normative appeal stems from the persuasiveness of the reasoning behind it. To give an example, the Brazilian Federal Supreme Tribunal (STF) has cited several times to Claus Roxin, a noted German scholar of criminal law, in just this way. In HC 92426/RS (2009), for instance, Minister Cezar Peluso argued in favor of a defendant who had stolen and used a check for the value of roughly 40 dollars (80 reais). Peluso appealed to the so-called insignificance principle, whose meaning he explained by tersely citing Roxin:

> This [principle], understood as a "regulative principle that preserves the integrity only of the area of punishability necessary for the protection of the legal good," [footnote reference to Roxin omitted] impugns de typicality of [i.e. the application of the statutory definition of the offense to] the conduct, which is to say that when the fact is not capable of concretely harming the protected legal good, it lacks one of the elements of the crime. The fact, thus, is not typical (My translation).

Consider also how laconically (often without even a quotation) the Supreme Court of Canada allows itself to refer to the work of Peter Hogg, a noted constitutional scholar:

> The focus of s. 15(1) is on *preventing* governments from making distinctions based on enumerated or analogous grounds that have the effect of perpetuating disadvantage or prejudice or imposing disadvantage on the basis of stereotyping. The focus of s. 15(2) is on *enabling* governments to pro-actively combat discrimination. Read thus, the two sections are confirmatory of each other. Section 15(2) supports a full expression of equality, rather than derogating from it. "Under a substantive definition of equality, different treatment in the service of equity for disadvantaged groups is an expression of equality, not an exception to it": P. W. Hogg (2007), *Constitutional law of Canada* (5th edn. Supp.), vol. 2, at p. 55–53 (*R v Kapp*, [2008] 2 S.C.R. 483, para 37).

And in a different case:

> The government argues that courts have no power under the Constitution of Canada to require the executive branch of government to do anything in the area of foreign policy. It submits that the decision not to request the repatriation of Mr. Khadr falls directly within the prerogative powers of the Crown to conduct foreign relations, including the right to speak freely with a foreign state on all such matters: Hogg PW(2007) *Constitutional law of Canada* (5th edn. Supp.), at p 1–19. (*Canada (Prime Minister) v Khadr*, [2010] 1 S.C.R. 44, par. 33).[11]

---

[11] Frequently, references to Hogg may consist in indirect references to precedents or other mandatory sources which Hogg does no more than report in his work. But Hogg's books are not mere case reports or detached expositions of the relevant legislated norms. Hogg, like any other constitutional scholar, deals with complicated texts and attempts to impose rational order on often

In some jurisdictions, as I will explain later, judges also appeal to the brute fact of scholarly consensus in order to bolster their decisions. It is hard to believe that judges associate the normative appeal of scholarly opinion directly with the soundness of the reasoning behind it when they refer, not to scholarly argument, but to the mere fact that the opinion has received the widespread endorsement of scholars.

Comparative law also provides useful evidence. Consider, for instance, what Green has said in contrasting Scots and English law:

> It is a matter of practice that Scots courts will cite certain institutional writers, such as Stair or Erskine, and that they will give their views authority (*faute de mieux*), though that authority is unable to defeat any contrary statute or decision, or even a moderately strong argument of public policy. In English law, however, parallel writers have an even weaker status, even the revered Blackstone. The difference lies not in the comparative merits of the writer's accounts of their respective legal systems, but in the content-independent fact of differential recognition by their respective courts (2009, 18).

Green is suggesting that, if Blackstone and Stair's influence in English and Scots law (respectively) were simply a function of the persuasiveness of their arguments, then we should expect them (on the plausible assumption that their works are equally admired in the relevant jurisdictions) to receive a similar degree of deference. But Stair's opinions are accorded more weight in Scotland than Blackstone's opinions are accorded weight in England. A plausible explanation (indeed the one that Green suggests) is that the influence of these authors stems from the "content-independent fact" that there are judicial customs assigning (varying degrees of) importance to them.

There is another way to raise doubt about the possibility that legal scholarship may be used as a source of law. It is not grounded on a distinct argument that could be analyzed and rebutted; rather it consists on an assertion that, although unsupported by argument, has considerable intuitive appeal: "the doctrinal writer cannot claim to possess any formal, rule-based authority—she cannot make propositions of law true (the way legislators and judges can)" (Bódig 2010, 10). The first part of

---

(Footnote 11 continued)
elusive lines of precedent. In those cases, where law is not clearly settled, Hogg's opinions could serve as genuine sources of law (To be clear, no claim is being advanced here to the effect that Hogg's works *are in fact* sources of law in Canada (nor is it the case that Roxin is clearly a source of law in Brazil). I mention summary references to Hogg by the Supreme Court of Canada only to illustrate the type of evidence indicating that a work is being used as a source of content-independent reasons for action. The conclusion that Hogg is indeed a source of law in Canada would require further demonstration that his works are *systematically* treated by judges (or at least by Supreme Court justices) as sources of content-independent reasons. Recall that, for Hart, a *practice*—which implies some degree of constancy on the part of those who participate in it— has to be disseminated among senior legal officials for it to constitute part of the rule of recognition. To establish that Hogg is a source of law in Canada I would need, thus, to show not only that he has been used a source of content-independent reasons on occasion but that he is used as such in systematic fashion. The same sort of proviso applies to all references made to Canadian judicial decisions in this work.)

this claim is not significantly different from Rubin's: scholars do not have the same sort of authority that legislators and judges do. But the second part is different. It appeals to legal semantics, contending that scholars cannot make legal propositions true: e.g., the fact that a scholar said that X is legally required cannot make "X is legally required" true. This may sound intuitively right, but it is really fraught with theoretical problems.

To begin, despite the normal implications of the choice of the word "cannot", it is more charitable to understand the claim as an empirical one: for there is no reason to believe that a scholar's say-so cannot conceivably make true a proposition of law. All it takes for that to be the case is the existence of a rule of recognition, of an official consensus, according to scholars that ability. This is perfectly conceivable.

As an empirical claim it also has problems. For what is a legal proposition? The example used above, "X is legally required", is arguably only one possible form of legal proposition. Indeed, it is a form of legal proposition that appears crude and uninformative to someone who is aware of the distinction between mandatory and permissive sources of law and of the fact that even the reasons deriving from mandatory sources are defeasible (albeit less easily defeated). Consider a different kind of proposition: "Judges have a defeasible legal reason to enforce X", Is the latter sort of proposition any less "legal" than the former sort? If it is legal, then why would one think that, as a matter of fact, scholars are never capable of making it true? Later in this chapter I will argue for the empirical thesis that scholarship functions as a permissive and less frequently also as "should-source" (sometimes generating very strong "shoulds") in modern legal systems. Thus, I will argue that scholars' says-so sometimes does make true legal propositions about what judges have content-independent reason to do. Right now, all that needs to be pointed out is that the intuitive appeal of the claim that scholars cannot make legal propositions true appears to rest on a conception of legal proposition that is only aware of mandatory sources (recall Bódig's reference to legislators and judges) and that ignores the phenomenon of the defeasibility of legal reasons.

I hope enough has been said to show that there is no general reason to doubt legal scholarship's capacity to function as a source of law. In the remainder of this chapter I will offer some general statements describing the ways in which legal scholarship currently figures in judicial argument in modern municipal legal systems.[12] These statements are intrinsically interesting but they should also serve as means for the construction of a case against an existing tendency to downplay the importance of legal scholarship as a source of law. This tendency—which does

---

[12] Although I focus on municipal legal systems, the role played by legal scholarship in the creation of international law is also a topic deserving of attention: "I submit that states really never make international law on the subject of human rights. It is made by the people that care; the professors, the writers of textbooks and casebooks, and the authors of articles in leading international law journals. If you go to the State Department and they have a question, where do they find the answer? If they find it in Ms. Whiteman's Digest, they consider that they have solved the problem" (Sohn 1995, 399).

not always emerge explicitly in the writings of philosophers but nevertheless seems to lurk behind their lack of interest in the topic of legal scholarship as a source of law—appears to be motivated by a conjunction of two beliefs: namely, that legal scholarship can only play the role of a permissive source of law, and that permissive sources are not deserving of attention.

The first conjunct, I will argue, is false (this would be enough, of course, for the entire conjunction to be rendered false, but I think it pays to consider the second conjunct as well). The second conjunct cannot be assessed in such a straightforward manner, but I believe it is motivated by a lack of appreciation of the interesting and informative ways in which legal scholarship figures in legal argumentation (even when it is no more than a permissive source). I will address the conjuncts in reverse order.

As stated earlier, there are different features of scholarship that may explain its status as a source of law. The fact that an article was published in a particular journal (or a book by a particular publishing company), the fact that its author is associated with a particular university, and the very name of the author are among the most common reasons why officials regard the opinions contained in scholarly writings as deserving of special attention. For instance, studies of the citation practices of American courts have suggested a clear judicial preference for articles appearing in prestigious law reviews, such as the *Harvard Law Review*, *The Yale Law Journal* and others (Sirico and Margulies 1986, 132; Merritt and Putnam 1996, 890). In England, to give another example, even when the curious convention against the citation of living authors still had significant force, authors such as Frederick Pollock and Arthur Goodhart were held in high regard among judges (Duxbury 2001, 84–101).

In civil law jurisdictions another interesting convention exists. In Brazil there is a common expression among lawyers which might be translated as "the doctrine of the majority".[13] It is fairly common for lawyers and professors to dismiss a point of view on a legal matter by associating it with the doctrine of the minority, and, on the other hand, to bolster an alternative opinion by associating it with the doctrine of the majority. Apparently the mere fact that a point of view is popular among scholars makes it presumptively more reliable than unpopular or unusual views (the burden of argument, which can be quite heavy, lies with the dissenting scholars). This convention, to be sure, is not entirely independent from the conventions that assign special importance to the writings of noted scholars, or to writings associated with particular journals, universities and publishing companies. For civilian lawyers are not undiscriminating with respect to the class of scholarly writings from which the relevant majority is to be drawn: their arguments refer to views widely shared by those scholars that, say, have acquired a certain prestige or that occupy senior positions in reputable universities.

It is not only in civil law jurisdictions that the consensus of respected writers can be used to bolster an argument (although professionals in those jurisdictions

---

[13] Similarly, Germans speak of the "dominant opinion" (Markesinis 1986, 352).

appear to be especially explicit and constant in appealing to this convention). Indeed, consider some decisions by the Supreme Court of Canada. In *Re B.C. Motor Vehicle Act*, Lamer J. states that "[i]t is now generally accepted among penologists that there are five main objectives of a penal system: see Nigel Walker, *Sentencing in a Rational Society*, 1969. ... Apart from death, imprisonment is the most severe sentence imposed by the law and is generally viewed as a last resort...." ([1985] 2 S.C.R. 486, par. 126) Similarly, in *Charkaoui v Canada*, McLachlin C.J. affirms that "[t]he use of special advocates has received widespread support in Canadian academic commentary. Professor Roach, for example, criticizes the Court of Appeal's conclusion in *Charkaoui (Re)*, 2004 FCA 421, that such a measure is not constitutionally required...." ([2007] 1 S.C.R. 350, para 82) In *R v Kapp*, MacClachlin C.J. and Abella J., in proposing that the earlier case of *Andrews v Law Society of British Columbia* provides a better analysis of the concept of substantive equality than the more recent *Law v Canada*, support their very short argument with two lengthy footnotes listing numerous scholarly works in which *Law*'s account of equality in terms of human dignity is criticized for being cumbersome and conducive to formalism ([2008] 2 S.C.R. 483, para 22, footnotes 1 and 2). The argument, to be clear, rests on little more than an imposing list of names.[14]

It is not only interesting to consider what features of scholarly writings make them appealing to lawyers and judges but also the contexts in which such writings are likely to be used. Legal scholarship (MacCormick 1978, 120–122) and permissive sources generally (Hart 1961, 246; Gardner 1988) are often used when mandatory sources are not capable of providing a determinate solution to the case at hand. Scholarship can therefore serve a gap-filling function. And, interestingly, it can help judges fill gaps in a way that (at least for rhetorical purposes) attenuates the discretionary nature of the gap-filling enterprise. Instead of simply resorting to substantive arguments, judges may resort to substantive arguments (or more often simply to the conclusions of those arguments) as they have been articulated by respected scholars. Such scholars share with the judge the responsibility for filling in the gaps.[15]

Scholarship is also used, but for a different purpose, when mandatory sources issue clear and determinate norms. Permissive sources do not usually defeat mandatory sources: for instance, if there is a clear, not grossly inadequate (in a substantive sense) statute that disposes of a case, a scholarly opinion that is critical

---

[14] Bastarache J, concurring with the result reached by majority in *Kapp*, also appeals to scholarly consensus in his argument for a particular interpretation of section 25 of the Charter of Rights and Freedoms: "Practically all authors agree with the fact that s. 25 operates as a shield..." ([2008] 2 S.C.R. 483, para 94).

[15] MacCormick claims that common law judges who, in hard cases, justify their decisions on the basis of principles that have not been established by mandatory sources privilege principles that have been articulated in non-mandatory sources such as *obiter dicta* and respectable juristic writings. Judges avoid, to the extent that they can, resorting to principles hat have not yet been affirmed by *any* source of law.

of the statute is unlikely to prevail. So, when the law is clear, scholarly opinions are more often used as supplements, as significant ways of reinforcing opinions that already rest on fairly solid ground.[16] When drafting arguments, I would often hear from the clinical professors at law school that I should find some support in the doctrine to strengthen a case which seemed fairly well supported by statute or precedent: "Good: the Civil Code is on our side. Now see if you can include a sympathetic quote from Caio Mário or Silvio Rodrigues [prestigious private law scholars in Brazil]". The importance of these quotes for our case would obviously vary according to the conclusiveness of the norms associated with the mandatory sources; but even if the latter were clearly on our side, Caio Mário and Silvio Rodrigues could still give us some assistance. And of course, there was normally no need to quote their arguments at length. As genuine sources of law, their unmotivated opinions provided content-independent reasons for action.

There is no argument to be given in support of the view that these facts about the use of scholarship in legal argumentation are intrinsically interesting. They just seem interesting. But something can be said as to why they are informative. I have already suggested that legal argumentation is formalist. Judges and lawyers do not argue like political philosophers and social reformers. In law, argument is significantly constrained by conventions that limit the use of substantive considerations that would otherwise be deemed appropriate. A political philosopher is primarily worried about what political arrangements are just or fair or likely to maximize welfare. Judges and lawyers are usually also worried about these things, but they need to make their views consistent (or at least roughly coherent) with the applicable rules of positive law, many of which prescribe actions that conform imperfectly to their political aspirations.

One may be tempted to regard the use of permissive sources as a non-formalist, non-constrained part of legal argumentation. After all, judges have the *option* of using or dismissing permissive sources. But this is not accurate, for even in the domain of the permissive, judges tend to abide by conventions that reflect their formalist inclinations. Legal scholarship that can function as a source of law is picked out by appeal to easily identifiable features (name, institution, publisher) that have only an indirect connection to persuasiveness or quality of reasoning. The use of substantive argument is not an essential part of the practice of employing permissive sources. Indeed, permissive sources can be, and often are, used to mitigate the otherwise very apparent substantive nature of legal argument in hard cases. The upshot is that a closer inspection of the use of scholarship as a source of law reveals (or rather confirms) features of legal argumentation which

---

[16] For instance, in *Re B.C. Motor Vehicle Act* Lamer J quotes Glanville Williams on the topic of *mens rea* only to assert that "[t]his view has been adopted by this Court in unmistakable terms in many cases, amongst which the better known are *Beaver v. The Queen,* [1957] S.C.R 531, and the most recent and often quoted judgment of Dickson J. writing for the Court in *R. v. City of Sault Ste. Marie, supra.*" ([1985] 2 S.C.R 486, par. 72) It appears that the opinion of the noted Welsh scholar is only reinforcing what precedent by itself was already capable of establishing.

might be missed or underplayed by those who take a dismissive attitude with respect to the topic of permissive sources of law.[17]

Let us go back now to the first conjunct and consider whether it is true that legal scholarship can only serve as a permissive source of law. There is no reason to believe that there is a logical or conceptual or even an unavoidable practical impediment to legal scholarship performing the function of a mandatory source of law. For instance, it is quite conceivable that judges in a particular jurisdiction may see themselves as duty-bound to address the opinions of a particular author. It is clearly another question, however, whether this is likely to happen. Indeed, one would be hard-pressed to find clear examples of scholarly writings being used as mandatory sources of law in modern municipal legal systems.[18]

Recall, however, that between permissive and mandatory sources there seems to exist another category. Some sources *should* be used even if it is not the case that they must be used. Sources that should be used are not "mere" permissive sources: their absence in a judicial decision or in a lawyer's brief motivates criticism. Caio Mário and Silvio Rodrigues, those authors whom the clinical professors advised me to cite, were not being used quite as "should-sources." My impression back then was, and remains today, that we could use them, and that using them would make our case more compelling, but that if I reported back to the clinical professor informing him that Caio Mário and Silvio Rodrigues were not willing to assist, he would probably shrug his shoulders and proceed without very much reluctance (unless he had no other grounds on which to rest his case). In other circumstances, however, legal scholarship seems more important than that, and a lawyer's silence with respect to the relevant scholarly writings is not inconsequential. Duxbury speaks of how English judges (which, recall, have traditionally been reluctant to

---

[17] Merryman (1954) considers a more specific reason why authors may downplay the importance of permissive sources, apart from their failure to see how much can be learned through the study of those sources: "Thus it is said that only statutes and cases are produced by the authority of the government, by legislators and judges who are aware that they are engaging in a lawmaking process and who are in some sense responsible to those to whom the law will be applicable. This difference is supposed to be sufficiently great to justify classification of secondary authority in such a way as to suggest that it is clearly inferior as 'law' to statutes and cases" (ibid. 620). Merryman's own response to this view requires no supplementation: "It is obvious however that given the judicial practice of citing secondary authorities in opinions these works can and do play a part in the total legal process which is not greatly different from that played by primary materials. It is possible for cases to be decided, rules of law to be stated, lines of decision begun and perpetuated, solely on the authority of a textual treatment having its origins outside the judicial or legislative process" (ibid. 620).

[18] My point, to be clear, is exclusively about modern legal systems. Scholarly opinions seem to have functioned in the past as mandatory sources of law. Jestaz (2005, 124) describes a period in Roman history where the *jurisconsultes* (a class of jurists that differ significantly from the modern, university-based scholars) were empowered by the Emperor to emit opinions which the courts were required to enforce. Eventually, Jestaz suggests, these jurists acquired a status that was hard to distinguish from that of regular government officials: "… ces jurisconsultes perdent peu à peu leurs traits originaux pour devenir des rouages de l'État".

cite scholarly literature) will sometimes complain about a lawyer's omission in this regard:

> We noted earlier that when, in the early 1970s, Lord Denning expressed his disappointment with counsel for failing, in *White* v. *Blackmore*, to cite relevant academic commentary in the courtroom, he was rubbing against the grain of judicial convention. Today, his reproval would not be considered quite so radical. Over the past twelve years, failure of counsel to refer to relevant academic literature has been bemoaned by Lord Keith in *Rowling* v. *Takaro Properties*, by Peter Gibson LJ in *State Bank of India* v. *Sood* and by Lord Steyn in the Court of Appeal decision in *White* v. *Jones* (2001, 106, footnotes omitted).

Now, the isolated complaints of a few judges may not be enough to establish that legal scholarship is a genuine "should-source", for we lack evidence of how representative the attitudes of these few judges are in relation to the attitudes of their peers, whose opinions also matter for the purpose of assigning to something the status of a source of law. But there are other reports which perhaps provide stronger evidence than Duxbury's. In the 1960s Justice Peters of the California Supreme Court enjoined the bar to use certain juristic sources, and suggested that this was not only a matter of personal opinion but an injunction that accorded with the attitudes of the appellate courts in California: "You should never overlook the Restatement of the Law, even when it is contrary to decisions in this state. The appellate courts are always interested in the Restatement, and have even reversed prior decisions because of it" (cited in Merryman 1977, 405, footnote 17).[19]

Also writing in the 1960s, but this time about South African law, Hahlo and Kahn (1968) distinguish between binding authority and persuasive material, and list among the former legislation, judicial precedent, and Roman-Dutch law (ibid. 140). The last item in this list (which was to be applied, apparently non-optionally, in the absence of governing legislation or applicable precedent: ibid. 303) refers to the legal system operating in Holland during the seventeenth and eighteenth centuries. Being largely non-codified and lacking systematic law reporting, Roman-Dutch law was largely to be found in collections of opinions of eminent lawyers, treatises, legal dictionaries, and encyclopedias (ibid. 543–562).[20]

---

[19] Some people are reluctant to classify the Restatements as instances of scholarship. This reluctance stems from the fact that scholars are not the only ones involved in crafting the Restatements (judges and lawyers also play a role) and that the Restatements are not written in a very scholarly spirit: they are explicitly a political enterprise. I am not persuaded. It seems that part of the authority of the Restatements derives from the fact that they are the products of experts many of whom are academics; and I am also not troubled by the fact that the Restatements are clearly meant to have a direct impact (a "political" impact) on judicial practice; all standard scholarship more or less aims to have practical impact.

[20] Some of the works systematizing Roman-Dutch law were authored by so-called *institutional* writers. A similar figure exists in Scots law (recall Green's reference to Stair and Erskine). South African and Scots law are perhaps peculiar in explicitly recognizing certain writers (the institutional ones) as sources of law, even if they do so while affirming their hierarchical inferiority relative to legislation and precedent (see White and Willock 2007, 167–168).

A more contemporary American example is drawn from what Schauer has said about a particular book on evidence law and its use by the Massachusetts Supreme Judicial Court and the Massachusetts Appeals Court:

> The more there is an expectation of reliance on a certain kind of technical optional authority – it is virtually impossible to argue or decide an evidence case in the Massachusetts Supreme Judicial Court, for example, without referring to Liacos's *Handbook of Massachusetts Evidence* – the more an authority passes from optional to mandatory (2009, 82)

And in a footnote Schauer adds:

> Given that [Liacos's] book, in all of its editions, has been cited 894 times by the Massachusetts Supreme Judicial Court and the Massachusetts Appeals Court, it would be a brave (or foolhardy) lawyer who attempted to argue a point of evidence before one of those courts without dealing with what Liacos has to say on the issue. To say that the source is not a mandatory authority thus appears to be a considerable oversimplification (ibid. 82, footnote 48).

To give another example, the authors of *Interpreting Precedents* (1997), an impressive comparative study analyzing the use of precedent in eleven different jurisdictions (including European Community Law), indicate a number of factors that may affect the degree of bindingness of precedents. They list factors such as the hierarchical rank of the court issuing the decision, whether the decision is merely of a panel or by a full bench, the reputation of the court or judge writing the opinion, the presence or absence of dissent, the age of the precedent, and so on. In that long list they also include the question how well the precedent is accepted in academic writings. The latter factor does not have equal importance in all jurisdictions, but at least in Germany it appears to be quite important:

> According to the Federal Constitutional Court the academic critique of a decision is important for the question whether the confidence of the citizen in the continuance of adjudication is protected: "Moreover, the decision of the Great Panel was so heavily criticized that the unchanged continuance of this line of decision could not seem secured" (BverfGE 84, 212 (227)).
>
> The Federal Court of Justice as well has... regarded highly contested precedents as being of lower value. To overrule them, "far-reaching legal dogmatic doubts and the incoherence of the achieved results" (BGHZ 106, 169 (174)) are sufficient (Alexy and Dreier 1997, 35–36).[21]

In Germany, then, the fact that academics are largely critical of a precedent may diminish its capacity to bind judges, and it may even provide sufficient justification for its reversal or transformation.[22] The upshot of this assortment of examples

---

[21] With respect to the Federal Constitutional Court, Kommers has made an even stronger claim: "The work of academic lawyers carries as much if not more weight in the Basic Law's interpretation than judicial precedents... the 'ruling opinion'... in the literature takes pride of place in the interpretations of the Basic Law" (2006, 193).

[22] In Belgium, adverse reactions from academics are also recognized as playing a significant role in the reversal of precedents from the *Cour de Cassation* (though not the role of a sufficient condition for reversal) (Rorive 2006, 283–289).

(English, South African, Scottish, American, German, Belgian) is that legal scholarship is not used exclusively as a permissive source of law. It is also used as a "should-source" and sometimes, as Schauer's report indicates, that "should" is so strong that legal scholarship comes rather close to playing the role of a mandatory source.

Allow me briefly to consider a potential objection. One might, while conceding the points about the potential of legal scholarship made so far, want to insist that rarely will legal scholarship serve the function of a source of law (mandatory or otherwise) in the exact same sense that things like legislation and precedent do. A rule of recognition identifying legislation and precedent as sources of law typically takes a fairly general form, such that it lends authority to rules of law possessing the (again, quite general) features of being laid down by the appropriate agents (e.g. members of Parliament). Although I have been speaking as if "legal scholarship" (generally) could function as a source of law, it could be argued that usually the features that render scholarly writings reason-giving are much less general than the features that are relevant to the authority of legislation and precedent. Indeed, particular authors and particular journals (referred to by proper names) often qualify as sources of law in jurisdictions where little deference is given to scholarship more generally—recall, for example, that English judges deferred to certain living jurists even when the convention against the citation of living authors was in force.

Now, it is true that we would not expect a rule of recognition to use proper names when referring to standard sources of law (presumably the current US rule of recognition makes reference to the office of President, certainly not to Obama himself). But I do not know how important this fact is and whether its acknowledgement warrants any skepticism about assigning to legal scholarship the unqualified status of a source of law. Is there any principled reason to deny that a rule of recognition may identify *some* of the sources of law of the relevant legal system by means of proper names?

Moreover, it should be noted that England is probably an exceptional case. It is only because English judges adhered to a convention against the citation of living authors that we hesitate to claim that the English rule of recognition operating at the time recognized scholarship more generally (as opposed to the writings of specific authors like Goodhart and Pollock) as sources of law. There is, however, less reason to hesitate when other, less unusual practices are concerned. Although it is not implausible to say, for instance, that the Massachusetts Appeals Court maintains a rule of recognition identifying Liacos's book as a source of law, it is equally plausible to say that it maintains a rule of recognition that accords normative force to the opinions of any author whose credentials are comparable. The norm that Liacos ought to be heeded may be an implication of a more general rule of recognition delineating general features of scholarly writings that are currently satisfied by Liacos's writings and perhaps by no one else's. Determining the exact content of a rule of recognition is hardly ever an easy task. Names of authors, book titles and things like that admittedly tend to stand out in the judicial practice of using legal scholarship, but that does not mean that the rule underlying that practice inevitably makes use of the specific terms by means of which we, as observes of that practice, often identify the instances of legal scholarship that have the capacity to generate content-independent reasons for action.

References

Aarnio A (2011) Essays on the doctrinal study of law. Springer, Dordrecht

Alexy R, Dreier R (1997) Precedent in the Federal Republic of Germany. In: MacCormick N, Summers RS (eds) Interpreting precedents: a comparative study. Dartmouth, Aldershot

Bódig M (2010) Legal theory and legal doctrinal scholarship. Can J Law Jurisprud 23:483 (Lexis pagination in the text)

Dan-Cohen M (1992) Listeners and eavesdroppers: substantive legal theory and its audience. Univ Colorado Law Rev 63:569

Duxbury N (2001) Jurists and judges: an essay on influence. Hart Publishing, Oxford

Duxbury N (2008) The nature and authority of precedent. Cambridge University Press, New York

Farber D (2000) Do theories of statutory interpretation matter? A case study. Northwest Univ Law Rev 94:1409

Farrell I (2006) H. L. A. Hart and the methodology of jurisprudence. Texas Law Rev 84:983

Ferraz TS Jr (1998) Função Social da Dogmática Jurídica. Max Limonad, São Paulo

Flanders C (2009) Toward a theory of persuasive authority. Okla Law Rev 62:55

Friedman L (1998) Law reviews and legal scholarship. Denver Univ Law Rev 75:661

Gardner J (1988) Concerning permissive sources and gaps. Oxford J Legal Stud 8:457

Gordon R (1993) Lawyers, scholars, and the "middle ground". Mich Law Rev 91:2075

Green L (2009) Law and the causes of judicial decisions. Oxford legal research paper series. Paper No. 14/2009. Available at http://ssrn.com/abstract=1374608. Accessed on 20 November 2011

Guastini R (2011) Rule-scepticism restated. In: Green L, Leiter B (eds) Oxford studies in philosophy of law, vol 1. Oxford University Press, Oxford

Hahlo HR, Kahn E (1968) The South African legal system and its background. Juta, Capetown

Hart HLA (1961) The concept of law. Clarendon Press, Oxford

Jestaz P (2001) Doctrine e Jurisprudence: Une Liaison de 25 Siècles. Thémis, Oxford

Jestaz P (2005) Les Sources du Droit. Dalloz, Paris

Kommers D (2006) Germany: balancing rights and duties. In: Goldsworthy J (ed) Interpreting constitutions. A comparative study. Oxford University Press, Oxford

Kötz H (1990) Scholarship and the courts: a comparative survey. In: Clark DS (ed) Comparative and private international law: essays in honor of John Henry Merryman on his seventieth birthday. Duncker & Humblot, Berlin

Kress K (1989) Legal indeterminacy. Calif Law Rev 77:283

Lacey N (2006) A life of H. L. A. Hart. The nightmare and the noble dream. Oxford University Press, New York

MacCormick N (1978) Legal reasoning and legal theory. Clarendon Press, Oxford

MacCormick N (1993) Argumentation and interpretation in law. Ratio Juris 6:16

Markesinis B (1986) Conceptualism, pragmatism and courage: a common lawyer looks at some judgments of the German Federal Court. Am J Comp Law 34:349

Merritt D, Putnam M (1996) Judges and scholars: do courts and scholarly journals cite the same law review articles? Chicago Kent Law Rev 71:871

Merryman JH (1954) The authority of authority: what the California supreme courst cited in 1950. Stanford Law Rev 6:613

Merryman JH (1977) Toward a theory of citations: an empirical study of the citation practice of the California Supreme Court in 1950, 1960, and 1970. South Calif Law Rev 50:381

Nino CS (1974) Consideraciones sobre la Dogmática Jurídica. UNAM, México

Peczenik A (1985) Moral and ontological justification of legal reasoning. Law Philos 4:289

Posner R (2002) Legal scholarship today. Harvard Law Rev 115:1314

Prakken H, Sartor G (2004) The three faces of defeasibility in the law. Ratio Juris 17:118

Rakoff T (2002) Symposium: law, knowledge, and the academy: introduction. Harvard Law Rev 115:1278

Rhode D (2002) Legal scholarship. Harvard Law Rev 115:1327

Rorive I (2006) Towards principles of overruling in a civil law supreme court. In: Endicott T et al (eds) Properties of law. Essays in honour of Jim Harris. Oxford University Press, Oxford

Ross A (1959) On Law and Justice (trans: Dutton M). University of California Press, Berkeley

Rubin EL (1988) The practice and discourse of legal scholarship. Mich Law Rev 86:1835

Rubin EL (1992) What does prescriptive legal scholarship say and who is listening to It: a response to professor Dan-Cohen. Univ Colorado Law Rev 63:731

Saks M et al (1994) Is there a growing gap among law, law practice, and legal scholarship? A systematic comparison of law review articles one generation apart. Suffolk Univ Law Rev 28:1163

Schauer F (1985) Easy cases. South Calif Law Rev 58:399

Schauer F (1991) The authority of legal scholarship. Univ Pennsylvania Law Rev 139:1003

Schauer F (2009) Thinking like a lawyer. A new introduction to legal reasoning. Harvard University Press, Cambridge

Schlag P (1992) Writing for judges. Univ Colorado Law Rev 63:419

Sirico LJ, Margulies J (1986) The citing of law reviews by the supreme court: an empirical study. UCLA Law Rev 34:131

Sohn L (1995) Sources of international law. Georgia J Int Comp Law 25:399

Solum L (1988) On the indeterminacy crisis: critiquing critical dogma. Univ Chicago Law Rev 54:462

Solum L (2006) Blogging and the transformation of legal scholarship. Wash Univ Law Rev 84:1071

Tushnet M (1987) Legal scholarship in the United States: an overview. The Mod Law Rev 50:804

Wendel B (2011) Explanation in legal scholarship: the inferential structure of doctrinal legal analysis. Cornell Law Rev 96:1035

White R, Willock I (2007) The Scottish legal system, 4th edn. Tottel, Edinburgh

Chapter 5
Formalism and the Use of Legal Scholarship

5.1 Formalism and Lack of Reference to Legal Scholarship

Comparative lawyers have associated lack of judicial reference to legal scholarship with judicial self-effacement. Duxbury, for instance, believes that one of the reasons behind the English convention against the citation of living authors was the so-called "declaratory theory" of law, a theory according to which judges never make new law themselves but simply apply existing law to situations which may not already have been officially dealt with (2001, 67). In a review of Duxbury's book Waddams elaborates the association thus:

> The attitude of English judges to judicial law-making tended, in the nineteenth century and for most of the twentieth, to suppress the element of personal judgment. The reluctance to acknowledge academic influence was a necessary consequence of this attitude, and demonstrates not so much a disparagement of academic work as an ostensible exclusion of all sources of influence of personal opinion. With the more open acknowledgment, throughout the common law world, of the importance of personal judicial opinion, it is natural for academic works, like other non-judicial sources, to be cited more frequently (2002, 307).

Similarly, Kötz associates lack of judicial reference to scholarship with what he calls "positivism": "Where positivism reigns and judges think that the law can be deduced from existing statutes or precedents, academic speculation on the interests and policies involved will be in lesser demand than where lawyers feel that legal rules must stand the test of functional adequacy in terms of contemporary values" (1990, 195).[1]

---

[1] It is fairly clear that, in using the term "positivism", Kötz is not referring to the jurisprudence of such authors as Hans Kelsen and H.L.A. Hart, since *their* positivism is not a normative theory of adjudication (that encourages judicial self-effacement or makes any other kind of recommendation to judges) but a non-normative theory of legal validity. Like Kötz, Vogenauer (2006, 879) also associates a conception of sources of law that excludes legal scholarship and other secondary authorities with "positivism". Merryman and Pérez-Perdomo (2007, 23) associate such a narrow conception of sources of law with "state positivism", although (as the qualifier "state" indicates) they put more emphasis on the fact that the admitted sources are directly associated with agents of the state than on the element of judicial self-effacement. In some jurisdictions judges may refrain from referring to scholarship not only, or not primarily, to suppress the element of personal judgment but because they hold the view that only the state, through its officials, can exercise law-making power.

F. P. Shecaira, *Legal Scholarship as a Source of Law*,
SpringerBriefs in Law, DOI: 10.1007/978-3-319-00428-0_5,
© The Author(s) 2013

Discussing the reluctance of the French *Cour de Cassation* to refer to scholarship, Kötz affirms that "[i]ts opinions shun the appearance of being the work of judges of flesh and blood who ever indulged in the luxury of doubt… a judgment should appear as a kind of surgical operation leading to the result by way of a simple, clear-cut deduction from premises stated in the form of an abstract principle, normally drawn from a statute" (Ibid. 186).

The idea seems to be that for the judge to resort to legal scholarship (and to other non-standard sources) is for him avowedly to include in his decision an element of personal judgment; it is for him to admit somehow to contributing to the creation or alteration of law (as opposed to the mere application of existing law). To me, the reasons why this association is made are not entirely clear. And to the extent that they can be understood, they are not very convincing.

Kötz, for instance, by emphasizing the positivists' rejection of "academic speculation *on the interests and policies* involved", seems to ignore or at least downplay the formalist character of standard legal scholarship, i.e. the kind of scholarship that speaks to judges and does not ignore their unwillingness to depart too sharply or too frequently from rules of positive law. It is quite true that judicial resort to critical legal theory, for instance, would likely be associated with judicial activism; but that is beside the point, for there is nothing standard about critical legal scholarship. The point is that Kötz only identifies a plausible connection between self-effacement and lack of citation to non-standard scholarship. Standard scholarship, i.e. the kind which is more likely to be heeded and effectively used by judges, is not addressed.

Waddams, on the other hand, apparently grounds the association between lack of reference to scholarship and judicial self-effacement on a general skepticism about scholarship's capacity to function as a genuine source of law[2]:

> Judges, as academics must surely concede, cannot with propriety *defer* to academic writing, as though a judge could say, "I cannot understand this article, but my clerk tells me it is very good" or, "it is written by a professor at Cambridge, so I must accept its conclusions"; academic writing can only properly be influential by having a persuasive effect on the mind of the judge, and such an effect is not felicitously called "authoritative." Constitutionally, judicial reasons must be the personal responsibility of the judge; academics may reasonably aspire to be helpful friends to the judges, but not authorities (2002, 306).

It appears that, for Waddams, legal scholarship can only have a persuasive function, and that when judges refer to it they are not relying on rules laid down by others (in this case by scholars) but are in effect engaging in the same sort of substantive reasoning that the scholars have engaged in. It should be clear to the

---

[2] This interpretation of Waddams is offered tentatively, as his comments are brief and superficial (and understandably so, given that they are part of a short book review). If I have got Waddams wrong, what follows may still serve a useful purpose as an assessment of a hypothetical reason for making the association between lack of reference to scholarship and judicial self-effacement. The association is undoubtedly made by Waddams and other authors; the tricky thing is to understand exactly what motivates it.

reader by this point that I do not agree with the first part of Waddams's claim (namely, that scholarship can only serve a persuasive function); scholarship can function as a genuine source of law, and when it does, it issues content-independent reasons for action. Waddams provides little argument for his position apart from the claim that it is something that "academics must surely concede". Well, I for one do not concede, and my reasons were given in the previous chapter. Even if I were to give Waddams the point, however, the association with self-effacement would remain dubious, as the soundness of a scholar's reasoning (if, again, we are focusing on standard legal scholarship) does not necessarily depend exclusively on the soundness of his substantive reasoning. Judges who are attracted by the persuasiveness of (standard) scholarly writings can apply them upon being persuaded by their technical, formalist arguments. The use of legal scholarship, even when it has a persuasive role, does not always open the door to substantive reasoning.

To recapitulate: the point so far is that it is not obvious why judges who believe in or advocate the declaratory theory of law or, relatedly, who want to efface traces of personal judgment from their decisions, would avoid making reference to (standard) legal scholarship. However, authors like Duxbury, Kötz, and Waddams have suggested that a self-effacing judge would avoid citing scholarly writings. Apparently the reason for this is that use of scholarly writings opens the door to substantive, non-formalist reasoning. I have already said why this claim is dubious. In the next section I will provide considerations that should help to weaken it even further. In the remainder of this section, in order to prepare some of the conceptual equipment that will be needed in the next section, it will pay to spend some time discussing the related notions of judicial self-effacement, substantive reasoning, and formalism.

In the previous chapter formalism was characterized as a general feature of legal argumentation. Compared to ordinary moral and political argumentation, all legal argumentation is formalist, given its extraordinary reliance on rules derived from conventional sources. To be clear, formalism comes in degrees, and when we compare the approaches of judges in different jurisdictions, or even judges within the same jurisdiction, we often observe differences with respect to how formalist they are. Some judges, while abiding by formal rules most of the time, are more willing to resort to substantive arguments than others: i.e. they are more willing to deviate from unsatisfactory rules and less concerned about establishing strong connections between the substantive considerations on which they rely and the rules which they do not strictly apply. Judges such as these are less formalist than they could be, although they certainly do not argue as freely as, say, moral and political thinkers do.

It is hard to provide a general explanation of why judges are formalist. Often formalism may be simply a product of indoctrination. In law school I was taught to regard law as a technical trade. I was never explicitly told to regard it as such, but since very early I was bombarded with endless, and endlessly intricate, rules and doctrines. It quickly became clear that obtaining highly coveted jobs like that of judge or public prosecutor depended on passing exams that focused almost exclusively on testing one's knowledge of formal rules and doctrines. The implicit suggestion, which my peers and I readily accepted, was that all our time and energy was to be spent in trying to understand those rules and doctrines and their interrelations. That was the purpose of law school; substantive issues, although addressed superficially from time to time, were not strictly within our province. The university had other departments for that: political science, economics, philosophy.

If my experience is representative, and it seems representative at least of legal education in civil law countries,[3] then it may be that many judges and practitioners acquire and maintain their formalist tendencies without much reflection. Applying formal rules is just what they are trained to do. A number of judges and practitioners may be able to free themselves from the fetters of indoctrination. In that case, their formalism, if they do not relinquish it, will be motivated either by a conviction that important substantive values are promoted if the law is effectively applied or, alternatively, by less noble, self-serving concerns (think of the judge who conforms in order to retain his position, prestige and salary or the lawyer who is concerned with winning cases by telling formalist judges what they want to hear). In the latter case, formalist rhetoric will not be entirely sincere: judges and practitioners' professed allegiance to the law will not quite match their private egoistic concerns.

What is interesting to note is that, whatever the motivation behind formalism, it usually contains a fairly explicit element of self-effacement. Whether they think it is simply their job to do so, whether they think it is the substantively right thing to do, or whether they conform out of self-interest, judges 'go on applying (or claiming to apply) formal rules and thus refraining (or claiming to refrain) from giving their personal, all-things-considered opinions about how best to solve particular legal issues. For the most part, it is *the law's* say-so that matters, not the judge's say-so.

So there is indeed an important connection between formalism and self-effacement: self-effacing judges do tend toward formalism. And I have also claimed that there is a crucial connection between formalism and the avoidance of substantive arguments (indeed, I define formalism as an argumentative approach

---

[3] Consider what Markesinis (2000, 297) has to say about legal education in Germany: "... at law school, the aspiring German judge will be taught how to use the codes, learn how to inter-link their various parts (and then combine the Codes with one another) and to begin at least to apply the texts he has been taught deductively. In all this, he will be expected to make as logical and as consistent a use as he can of the many concepts that will be drummed into his head during a period of at least seven... years of training". Generally, common lawyers are more reluctant to describe their own education in this way, but there are some who are not: "Law school tries to empty the mind of all 'extraneous' matter, the better to develop legal skills". (Friedman 1986, 774) "Prestigious law schools offer courses in sociology, history, or philosophy of law; or in psychology or anthropology of law. But everybody knows that these are elegant frills, like thick rugs in the dean's office; they have nothing to do with 'real' legal education. A school can do without these frills, in a crunch. Indeed, being a frill is precisely what makes these courses valuable, even essential, to an elite law school" (Ibid. 777).

that significantly limits the use of substantive arguments). One may still have
doubts, however, about the existence of a significant connection between self-
effacement and the avoidance of substantive arguments. Formalism is self-effacing
insofar as its adherents attribute the decisions they make to the law, to formal legal
rules, and deny making any contribution by means of personal judgment. But
substantive arguments, one could argue, can also be presented in an impersonal
way. Take moral arguments, for instance. Ethicists (at least ethical realists)[4] do not
characterize their moral views as subjective or personal. They speak in terms of
morality's demands, or in terms of what is morally correct or reasonable, a rhetoric
that parallels formalist legal rhetoric ("the law [morality] demands that we Φ";
"Φ-ing is legally [morally] permissible").

The question, then, is: Why assume that moral arguments (and perhaps substantive arguments more generally) cannot be articulated in self-effacing fashion?
Well, there is no doubt that they can be so articulated. The problem is that not very
many people are willing to buy self-effacing rhetoric when it is used in the
articulation of moral arguments. In other words, there is much less cynicism about
the self-effacing pretensions of legal formalist rhetoric than there is about the self-
effacing pretensions of moral rhetoric that emphasizes the demands of morality as
an impersonal set of rigid rules. Jurists usually see through the rhetoric in the latter
case. So, going back to an earlier point, I submit that Kötz and Waddams were not
wrong to suggest that judges avoid resorting to moral arguments in order to
suppress the element of personal judgment. For they, the judges, and their readership tend to associate moral argument and personal judgment. What I have
criticized is Kötz and Waddams' belief that judges also avoid resorting *to scholarly writings* in order to suppress the element of personal judgment; this is a
dubious contention which I will continue to discuss in the next section.

For now, let me explain in more detail why it can indeed be hard to buy self-
effacing rhetoric in the domain of moral argument. It would be rash to claim that
we live in an age of moral skepticism. On the contrary, if I had to venture a guess I
would say that moral realism is more widespread. Evidence that I am not alone in
this regard is provided by the fact that, in metaethics, skeptics are usually assigned
a heavy burden of argument (a burden which skeptics themselves often accept).
That burden is assigned precisely because, by denying the existence of moral facts
and/or the possibility of moral knowledge, skeptics fail to vindicate realist
assumptions that appear to shape ordinary moral discourse and practice.[5]

---

[4] Ethical realists, as I am using the expression, make at least three distinct claims: (i) that moral
statements are truth-apt; (ii) that some moral statements are true; and (iii) that we, even as
imperfect reasoners, can identify some of those true moral statements.

[5] Error theorists in particular have been quite ready to accept such a burden. See, for instance,
Mackie (1977, 35): "But since this is an error theory; since it goes against assumptions ingrained
in our thought and built into some of the ways in which language is used, since it conflicts with
what is sometimes called common sense, it needs very solid support;" and Joyce (2001, 135): "A
proponent of an error theory—especially when the error is being attributed to a common, familiar
way of talking—owes us an account of why we have been led to commit such a fundamental,

But moral argument has other, widely recognized features that are not easily squared with its admittedly realist tendencies. Non-trivial moral questions whose resolution does not depend on the settlement of non-moral (e.g. sociological, psychological, historical) issues tend to generate pervasive and intractable disagreement. I have in mind the sort of disagreement that stems from divergence with respect to moral intuitions for which little argument can be given. Allow me to provide, for the purpose of illustration, some assorted examples of contentious moral intuitions that give rise to intractable disagreement: autonomy (as distinct from more tangible manifestations of well-being) is a good; life has intrinsic value; human life is more valuable than non-human life; the rights of actual persons have priority over those of potential persons (e.g. fetuses, future generations); we have duties toward our kin that have priority over our duties toward strangers; certain acts should be deemed supererogatory and hence morally optional, i.e. neither required nor forbidden (different ethicists intuitively draw the line between the required and the supererogatory in different ways); there is something unfair about a society that does nothing to mitigate the economic gap that tends to appear between the naturally talented or entrepreneurial and the naturally untalented or unadventurous; some wrong-doers deserve punishment even when punishment will serve no deterrence function; defamation can (in and of itself) harm an individual who is entirely ignorant of it.

The list could continue indefinitely. Indeed, I have not mentioned any of the countless examples of conflicts of intuitions pertaining not to the assertion of rights and duties, or to the ascription of value to certain states of affairs, but to the proper way of adjudicating possible conflicts between rights, duties or values that are equally endorsed by the relevant arguers. So, for instance, two arguers who agree that governments ought to protect certain individual rights as well as promote general welfare can still disagree (on the basis of little more than intuition) about when welfare considerations are pressing enough to justify the infringement of individual rights.[6]

Some of the contentious intuitions mentioned above are perhaps of interest only to professional philosophers. Others, however, will also capture the attention of thoughtful laypersons. For some of those intuitions are responsible, for instance, for the divide between liberals and conservatives, a pervasive divide which runs through plural societies and deeply affects the lives of citizens and officials (including, naturally, judges). Such is the nature of the divide that when liberals

---

(Footnote 5 continued)

systematic mistake". Error theorists typically hold the view that moral statements are truth-apt while insisting that they are all false (given that the facts which they purport to describe do not exist). Not all skeptics are error theorists, of course, but their views are also counter-intuitive insofar as they deny any one of the three realist claims (note 4 *supra*) that appear to shape ordinary moral discourse.

[6] In Canada, the Supreme Court faces this problem virtually every time it considers whether the violation of a Charter right is justifiable under section 1 of the Canadian Charter of Rights and Freedoms.

and conservatives disagree about an important policy matter, there can usually be little hope that they will come to an agreement by any means other than the counting of hands. And, it should be emphasized, this will be the case even if we are thinking of well-informed, well-intentioned liberals and conservatives. It is not to the antagonistic nature of partisan politics that I am alluding here; it is rather to the inconclusive nature of much moral argument.

It has been argued persuasively that the existence of intractable moral disagreement is not a good enough reason for the rejection of moral realism. This is mainly because *at most* moral realism requires that most moral disputes be resolvable *in principle*: disagreement that is currently intractable may still be resolvable in ideal circumstances, where arguers are fully informed, fully rational, and free from time constraints (Brink 2009, 199). My purpose, however, is not to show that the existence of intractable moral disagreement establishes the falsity of moral realism, but only that it plausibly explains an existing cynicism with respect to self-effacing moral claims when they are made by judges. Judges are by no means experts about the non-trivial moral issues which they often have to settle, and they inevitably work under significant time constraints and other institutional pressures. Thus, when judges pronounce on contentious moral matters, it strikes many as naive to conclude that they are simply abiding by dictates whose validity they perceived through rational deliberation. The conclusion at which many scholars arrive is that judges are not compelled by reason to arrive at their moral positions (for judges can hardly argue in defense of the contentious intuitions grounding those positions) but rather that judges decide moral issues in accordance with their subjective preferences. So far as reason and argument are concerned, they could have gone either way. They do not *reason* to their final positions; in a sense, they *choose* them. It is, I submit, the perception that the possibility of choice is significantly increased in the domain of moral argument (compared to that of legal argument) that explains cynicism with respect to self-effacing rhetoric in that domain.

At the risk of being repetitive, let me emphasize what has been argued so far. Self-effacing judges tend toward formalism. And they also tend to avoid appealing to moral argument to the extent that they can. For they know that, even if they dress up their moral arguments in self-effacing language, they are likely to be seen as engaging in activism. Kötz and Waddams (and the other authors I have mentioned in this section) are with me so far. We disagree only with respect to the further view that self-effacing judges also tend to avoid using legal scholarship. I will continue to pursue this issue in the following section.

5.2   Challenging the Association

Schauer (1988) helpfully distinguishes between two senses of formalism. There is formalism as the denial of choice (a denial which may or may not be sincere; and if sincere, may or may not be the product of self-deception); and there is formalism as the actual exercise of self-restraint, i.e. the honest and effective disposition to abide by rules prescribing determinate courses of action. It is in the first sense, Schauer argues, that the US Supreme Court's decision in the controversial case of *Lochner v New York* has been described as formalist. In that case, the Court held that liberty of contract (in particular, the liberty to have a baker work for an extended number of hours regardless of health-related concerns) was implicit in the due process clause of the Fourteenth Amendment. Schauer comments on the rhetoric of the majority opinion:

> Justice Peckham's language suggests that he is explaining a precise statutory scheme rather than expounding on one word in the Constitution [i.e. "liberty"]. It is precisely for this reason that his opinion draws criticism. We condemn *Lochner* as formalistic not because it involves a choice, but because it attempts to describe this choice as compulsion. What strikes us clearly as a political or social or moral or economic choice is described in *Lochner* as definitionally incorporated within the *meaning* of a broad term. Thus, choice is masked by the language of linguistic inexorability (Ibid. 511–12, reference omitted).

So *Lochner* denied choice. But people see through the rhetoric. Legal formalist rhetoric is always subject to the sort of criticism that has been directed at *Lochner*: for claiming to abide by a formal rule of law is not necessarily equivalent to abiding by it. I argued in the previous section not that legal formalist rhetoric never misleads (i.e. never obscures the exercise of choice that in fact takes place) but that it is normally accepted at face value with less reluctance than the self-effacing moral rhetoric that judges may also employ.

The question that remains is whether it is right to affirm, as some authors have, that judges wishing to deny that they are making choices, i.e. judges employing self-effacing rhetoric, tend to avoid making reference to legal scholarship. I have already shown some reason to regard this claim as dubious. I will attempt to strengthen the case against it in this section by indicating a host of other reasons that can help to explain variations in judges' relation to scholarship.

Waddams was quoted earlier as saying that "[t]he attitude of English judges to judicial law-making tended, in the nineteenth century and for most of the twentieth, to suppress the element of personal judgment. The reluctance to acknowledge academic influence was a *necessary* consequence of this attitude". (emphasis added) So far, I have proceeded as if Waddams employed the term "necessary" loosely, i.e. as a synonym of "highly likely" or "very natural" or something else to that effect. For it is very implausible to claim that it would be incoherent for one to acknowledge academic influence while denying the element of personal judgment. Even if there were a natural tendency for self-effacing judges to avoid scholarship there still would be nothing strictly incoherent about a judge's attempt to suppress the element of personal judgment while openly relying on legal scholarship. For one thing, judges may restrict their references to scholarship to hard cases where the use of substantive argument is very hard to avoid anyway. In such cases, reference to scholarly authorities would actually serve the function of mitigating the discretionary nature of the judicial decisions: judges would not be filling in gaps on their own but would be relying on the assistance of experts. This is a way of showing (some degree of) deference and self-restraint. A Canadian case can be used to illustrate the point.

In *R v Morgentaler* Wilson J came to the conclusion that a criminal statute prohibiting abortions at all stages of pregnancy failed the proportionality test pertaining to section 1 of the Canadian Charter of Rights and Freedoms: "It [i.e. the criminal statute] is not sufficiently tailored to the legislative objective and does not impair the woman's right 'as little as possible'" ([1993] 3 S.C.R. 463, para. 259). Her argument for this position consisted in the contentious claim that,

> in balancing the state's interest in the protection of the foetus as potential life under s. 1 of the *Charter* against the right of the pregnant woman under s. 7 greater weight should be given to the state's interest in the later stages of pregnancy than in the earlier. The foetus should accordingly, for purposes of s. 1, be viewed in differential and developmental terms: see Sumner LW (1981), Professor of Philosophy at the University of Toronto, *Abortion and Moral Theory*, pp 125–128 (Ibid. para 257).

Notice how Wilson used scholarship in her opinion. She was clearly addressing a difficult moral question (are fetuses at later stages of the pregnancy more deserving of protection than fetuses at earlier stages?) which existing constitutional law did not answer with precision; and she attempted to make her own answer more credible by making summary reference to the opinion of an expert affiliated with a prestigious Canadian university.

That is just one way in which reference to scholarship may coherently be put to use by self-effacing judges. Another way of doing it can be gleaned from Markesinis's study of the German judicial style. Markesinis talks about the German judge's tendency toward highly abstract, conceptual reasoning. This tendency is connected to the German judge's readiness to engage carefully with complex academic theories. Someone who thinks like Waddams might be tempted to jump to the conclusion that these are signs that the German judge is *not* reluctant to avow his personal contributions. But that would go against Makesinis' account of the German judge's "codal background" and formalist training (2000, 297–298). Instead, Markesinis associates the German judge's fondness of abstract, complex theory with his distinctive "scientific" ambitions:

> A reader of German judgments expecting them to be abstract, conceptual and difficult to follow will, on the whole, not be disappointed in this expectation. Logic is often taken to extremes, legal details relentlessly pursued; as Harry Lawson once told me, "they leave nothing to the imagination."... [They] pursue relentlessly their scientific approach which (they are taught to believe) is bound to produce the right result and may even lead them into the Paradise of Legal Ideas (1986, 366).

This introduces an association not previously made in this book, at least not explicitly: legal scholarship need not be associated with contentious substantive argument and hence with personal judgment; in some legal cultures, it is rather associated with *science*. Indeed, "legal science"—*Rechtswissenschaft*—is another phrase commonly used in Germany and other Continental jurisdictions alongside "the doctrine" and "legal dogmatics". Scholars may be regarded as seeking rigor and precision even in domains where these goals are not easily attained. When

German judges, in their dialogue with scholars, present themselves as taking part in a scientific pursuit, they do not present themselves as engaging in a creative or discretionary enterprise. *Science* is a notion that, in Germany and elsewhere, connotes objectivity; and therefore it is a notion that can be co-opted for the purposes of self-effacing judges. To be sure, no one has to buy the objective pretensions of judicial scientific rhetoric (Markesinis himself has expressed reservations about German judges' reluctance to acknowledge their part in "social engineering": see 2000, 308). Again, all I am saying is that there is nothing incoherent about a judge using self-effacing rhetoric and yet referring to scholarly work.

Indeed, the history of German legal thought provides telling instances of a strong association between use of legal research and objectivity. It has been claimed that in the nineteenth century German legal theory was dominated by the so-called jurisprudence of concepts, a paradigmatic manifestation of formalism in legal thought. Adherents to the jurisprudence of concepts, the story goes, conceived of law as a closed and determinate set of propositions arranged in pyramid-like fashion, with an abstract principle or concept at the top from which all other propositions could ultimately be deduced (Larenz 1997, 24–27). It was importantly admitted by jurisprudents of concepts that legal norms do not spring to life through legislation and adjudication in complete, determinate, systematic form; statutes, precedents, and customs contain a multitude of elusive concepts whose meaning is to be determined and the logical relations among which are to be identified by legal scholars. Law is indeed a formal system but that is so thanks to the tireless conceptual labor of legal scholars. Conceived in this way, legal scholarship is a source of norms the use of which is by no means a way of admitting recourse to personal judgment: to have recourse to the pyramid of legal propositions constructed by scholars is to have recourse to a closed, complete system of norms—indeed, a formal system which, had it not been for scholars, would not be available to guide and constrain judges.

Let us now move on to the more plausible contention that there is a tendency, and perhaps a strong one, for judges who wish to suppress the element of personal judgment not to acknowledge scholarly influence. In the previous section I raised doubts about this claim by challenging assumptions apparently held by those who have made it. So, while both Kötz and Waddams apparently made the mistake of associating scholarly work with purely substantive argument (thus ignoring the importance of standard legal scholarship), Waddams apparently made the further mistake of denying that legal scholarship can serve the function of a genuine (content-independent-reason-giving) source of law. I now want to make a more positive contribution, by suggesting a number of factors that help to explain lack of judicial reference to academic writings. None of these factors has to do with a wish to efface traces of personal judgment from judicial decisions.

Before making my argument, I should draw attention to an important difference between the following questions, which have been lumped together up to this point: (1) what explains lack of judicial reference to scholarship? and (2) what explains judicial reluctance to acknowledge academic influence? The answers to these questions are not necessarily the same (although they should overlap to some extent), for judges may fail to refer to scholarship without this being a sign that they are *reluctant* to do so: they might indeed be happy to seek and acknowledge academic influence if only their circumstances were different (more will be said about these circumstances shortly). A Hartian might put the point slightly differently by saying that lack of reference to scholarship may be no more than a sign that judges are not in the habit of referring to scholarship. Obviously judges who are reluctant to acknowledge academic influence are also not in the habit of referring to scholarship, but presumably (for what else would justify the use of the term "reluctance?") they also display a certain normative attitude with respect to their behavior, at the very least a doubt as to whether they *ought to* be relying on scholarship. While acknowledging the difference between questions (1) and (2), I will try to show that in neither case it seems a good idea to give an answer that relies primarily on the self-effacing attitudes of judges. It is not a good idea when all we know is that judges lack the habit of referring to scholarship, and it is also not a good idea when we know that they believe they ought to avoid the habit (which they in fact lack). I will consider these two cases in reverse order.

The English convention against the citation of living authors is a good example of avowed judicial reluctance to acknowledge scholarly influence. Duxbury considers a number of reasons why English judges may have created and followed the convention (in addition to the previously discussed popularity of the declaratory theory of law).[7] For instance, English judges may have feared to offend "other living jurists who consider their own opinions to be just as authoritative and relevant as those [of the jurists actually cited]" (2001, 67). Also, "the convention may have been favoured in order to prevent or reduce judicial citation of immature or unreflective commentary". (Ibid. 67) Moreover, judges may have worried that "academic commentators are exempt from *stare decisis*. If commentary is recognized too hastily as work of authority, there is a risk that the author will change his or her mind and so render the source of law uncertain". (Ibid. 73).[8] Another

---

[7] Although I am no expert in the history of English law, it seems to me that Duxbury's belief in the popularity of the declaratory theory of law ("a theory which was subscribed to by many English judges certainly until the mid-twentieth century" (Duxbury 2001, 66)) should not be accepted without caution. There are studies making the conflicting claim that the declaratory theory met its demise in the nineteenth century (Evans 1987, 68; Bankowski et al. 1997, 482). Indeed, such studies suggest the existence of a link between the supposed demise of the declaratory theory and the introduction into the common law of the doctrine of *stare decisis* in its modern form (Duxbury raises doubts about this link in a recent book: Duxbury 2008, Chap. 2). Perhaps neither Duxbury nor the authors who would dispute his claim are entirely right. That is to say, the truth may lie somewhere between the two extremes: the declaratory theory may have had some (as opposed to pervasive) influence among English judges while the convention against the citation of living authors was still in force. The fact, however, that the declaratory theory may not have been as popular as Duxbury suggests serves to weaken even further the causal connection he postulates between that theory and the convention against the citation of living authors.

[8] In 1950 the Chief Justice of the Supreme Court of Canada precluded counsel from citing the *Canadian Bar Review* during oral submissions. According to Sharpe and Proulx (2011, 3), this attitude "was ostensibly grounded in the fear of relying on the works of living authors who might

reason, one which Duxbury finds especially interesting, is that "judges ought to be wary of relying on the works of living commentators… because the two groups inhabit distinct legal worlds and are engaged in very different enterprises" (Ibid. 74). Indeed, juristic reflection is not affected by the institutional and temporal constraints that impact judicial deliberation, and jurists do not have the benefit of forming an opinion in light of the focused debates that characterize litigation in adversarial systems (although one could argue that excessive focus on the particularities of concrete cases may also lead to skewed analyses and myopic conclusions).

Note that these are all plausible motivations for a convention restricting citation to legal scholarship; and note also that they are motivations that are unrelated to any judicial wish to suppress the element of personal judgment. Instead, they have to do with avoidable inconveniences (e.g. upsetting living authors whose works are being ignored) and with the dubious quality or usefulness to adjudication of the works of living authors and of legal scholarship generally. The alleged popularity of the declaratory theory, which to me still bears a mysterious relation to the avoidance of scholarship, is engulfed by the abundance of alternative reasons that may help to explain the convention against the citation of living authors: where scholarship is held in high regard and judges are not worried about oversensitive or fickle or high-flown authors, there would appear to be little reason for a convention restricting the use of scholarship.

Nicholls suggests a plausible historical explanation of the English convention which does not make any reference to the declaratory theory of law:

> The historic emphasis in England on case law and the rather grudging attitude, until recently, towards text writers are the two sides of a single coin, the special circumstances explaining the growth of the first also explaining the second. The English system of precedent was attributed by Sir John Salmond to "the peculiarly powerful and authoritative position which has been at all times occupied by English judges".... Sir William Holdsworth put essentially the same idea when he wrote that the method of developing law in England through the authority of decided cases "could only have been invented by a learned self-governing profession, responsible only to itself" and: "But even such a profession could not have developed this method of developing law if the Courts had not been staffed by an independent bench of judges, sufficiently well paid to secure that they were, as a general rule, more able than the bar.... A system of appointing judges which does not secure both the presence of the ablest lawyers on the bench and security of tenure will never be able to operate successfully our English system of case law". If we add the centralizing reforms of English kings in medieval times and the fact that even much later there were no teachers of English law at the universities, we shall have a fairly complete picture of the forces at work. These forces together no doubt made English judges in the past sensitive of the dignity of their position and ready on occasion to discourage incipient rivals (1950, 9–10, footnotes omitted).

(Footnote 8 continued)

later rescind or disavow their published statements". Sharpe and Proulx also speculate that "more fundamentally, the refusal to look beyond case law and statutes was a product of a highly formalist and anti-intellectual judicial culture…".

Where judges simply fail to refer to scholarship without giving any clear indication that they find the practice objectionable, worries about self-effacement also appear to be dispensable as an explanatory device. Lack of or limited use of scholarship can sometimes be explained by relatively prosaic factors like heavy workloads and limited resources: for a judge's ability to review the relevant scholarly writings requires not only a considerable amount of time but also access to updated libraries and electronic sources (Schwartz and Petherbridge 2011, 120–122), and ideally the assistance of knowledgeable clerks (Kötz 1990, 195). Lack of or limited use of scholarship can also be a function of the largely oral nature of the judicial process in some jurisdictions, where judges even at the appellate level may normally dictate brief decisions to clerks who transcribe and print them (Duxbury 2001, 68). And even where the judicial process is not predominantly oral, there often exists a tradition of terse judicial decisions (recall the case of France), decisions that are frugal about citing authorities in general[9] and consequently about citing typically permissive sources like scholarship.

Now, I have so far given reasons why judges in some jurisdictions may deliberately avoid or simply fail to engage in the habit of using scholarship. It could also be instructive, however, to consider whether judges in jurisdictions where scholarship is regularly used are distinctively unconcerned about allowing personal judgment to make itself apparent in their decisions. Presumably, if self-effacing tendencies explain avoidance of scholarship, then judges who lack such tendencies (or have them to a lesser degree) would be more likely to use scholarship, provided that they do not have countervailing reasons to avoid it (e.g. unreliable scholarly literature, lack of time and resources, etc.). I cannot currently disprove that there is a significant connection between use of scholarship and a lack of judicial worry about self-effacement. I can, however, offer a quick word about why attempts to prove that the connection does exist are unlikely to be successful.

In a word, reliable inter-jurisdictional comparisons are not easy to come by. American judges are traditionally less reluctant to use scholarship than English judges are, and the former are also traditionally less coy about avowing personal contributions (or at least about employing overtly substantive arguments; see Atiyah and Summers 1987) than the latter are. But one cannot conclude on this basis that their differences with respect to the use of scholarship are a function of their differences with respect to self-effacing attitudes. For the US and England traditionally differ in a number of other relevant respects: e.g. they are not equally oral legal cultures (Atiyah 1983, 549), they are not equal with respect to the availability of the relevant resources (ibid. 549), they have not always had equally

---

[9] The discourse of French judges is not only misleading with respect to the influence of scholarship on their decisions. Comparative lawyers have claimed that the lack of citation to precedent in high courts in France should not obscure the fact that French law "would be incomprehensible without reference to the precedents of higher courts filling gaps in or otherwise supplementing the codes and other formal legal sources". (Bankowski et al. 1997, 532) On the same point, see Bell (1997, 1248–1253).

vibrant and prestigious legal academic communities[10] (Atiyah and Summers 1987, 384–388), and so on.[11] To make an informative comparison we would need to select jurisdictions that are similar in all (or perhaps most) relevant respects except with regard to self-effacing attitudes. That requires a pair of jurisdictions that may not be very easy to find; at least authors like Duxbury, Waddams and Kötz have not presented it.

References

Atiyah P (1983) Lawyers and rules: some Anglo-American comparisons. South Law J 37:545
Atiyah P, Summers R (1987) Form and substance in Anglo-American law. Clarendon Press, Oxford
Bankowski Z et al (1997) Rationales for precedent. In: MacCormick N, Summers RS (eds) Interpreting precedents: a comparative study. Dartmouth, Aldershot
Bell J (1997) Book review: comparing precedents. Cornell Law Rev 82:1243
Braun A (2006) Professors and judges in Italy: it takes two to tango. Oxford J Legal Stud 26:665
Brink D (2009) Moral realism and the foundations of ethics. Cambridge University Press, Cambridge
Duxbury N (2001) Jurists and judges: an essay on influence. Hart Publishing, Oxford
Duxbury N (2008) The nature and authority of precedent. Cambridge University Press, New York
Evans J (1987) Change in the doctrine of precedent during the nineteenth century. In: Goldstein L (ed) Precedent in law. Clarendon Press, New York
Friedman L (1986) The law and society movement. Stanford Law Rev 38:763
Joyce R (2001) The myth of morality. Cambridge University Press, Cambridge
Kötz H (1990) Scholarship and the courts: a comparative survey. In: Clark DS (ed) Comparative and private international law: essays in honor of John Henry Merryman on his seventieth birthday. Duncker & Humblot, Berlin
Larenz K (1997) Metodologia da Ciência do Direito, 3rd edn. Calouste, José Lamego, trans. Lisboa
Mackie J (1977) Ethics: inventing right and wrong. Penguin, London
Markesinis B (1986) Conceptualism, pragmatism and courage: a common lawyer looks at some judgments of the German federal court. Am J Comp Law 34:349
Markesinis B (2000) Judicial style and judicial reasoning in England and Germany. Camb Law J 59:294
Merryman JH, Pérez-Perdomo R (2007) The civil law tradition. An introduction to the legal systems of Europe and Latin America, 3rd edn. Stanford University Press, Stanford
Nicholls GVV (1950) Legal periodicals and the supreme court of Canada. Can Bar Rev 28:422
Schauer F (1988) Formalism. Yale Law J 97:509
Schwartz D, Petherbridge L (2011) The use of legal scholarship by the federal courts of appeals: an empirical study. Cornell Law Rev 96:101

---

[10] It is interesting to note that while the existence of a vibrant academic community may serve as an incentive to judicial use of scholarship, academics may also become too influential or too prolific for the tastes of judges and other legal officials. Indeed, concerns of this nature are apparently behind Italian legislation prohibiting citation of legal writers by judges (Braun 2006, 671–675).

[11] For a detailed comparison of English and American courts as to matters bearing on the relationship between judges and jurists, see also Duxbury (2001), Chaps. 3 and 5.

Sharpe RJ, Proulx V-J (2011) The use of academic writing in appellate decision-making. Can Bus Law J 50:550

Vogenauer S (2006) Sources of law and legal method in comparative law. In: Reinmann M, Zimmermann R (eds) The Oxford handbook of comparative law. Oxford University Press, New York

Waddams S (2002) Book review: jurists and judges. An essay on influence by Neil Duxbury. Univ Toronto Law J 52:305

Chapter 6
Normative Questions

In this chapter, rather than providing precise answers to normative questions regarding the use of legal scholarship by judges, I will offer some general remarks about how such questions should be approached. There are two reasons to avoid making specific recommendations as to when (if ever) and how judges should use legal scholarship. For one thing, it is important enough to spend some time identifying potential mistakes in approach that could lead normative inquirers into making false starts. Moreover, appropriate answers to questions about when and how legal scholarship should be used vary significantly according to legal culture and (within a particular legal culture) court level or type of legal question. So, what we may want to recommend to judges in one jurisdiction will not always be recommendable to judges in a different jurisdiction. And (with regard to a particular jurisdiction) what we may want to recommend to judges in certain courts dealing with certain types of questions will not always be recommendable to judges in other courts facing different kinds of challenges.

Consider one kind of mistake in approach that normative inquirers should avoid. One might see questions about when and how judges ought to be using legal scholarship as directly related to questions about how much discretion, how much leeway or freedom of choice, judges should be permitted to have. However, this way of approaching normative questions about the use of legal scholarship is rendered dubious by the conclusions of the previous chapter. In that chapter I argued against the view that there is a tendency not to cite legal scholarship among judges who deny the exercise of choice or wish to efface the traces of personal opinion from their decisions. My claims apply equally to judges who employ self-effacing rhetoric sincerely, and thus honestly attempt to practice self-restraint, as well as to judges who deny choice while consciously exercising it. Judges who mislead their audience will not jeopardize their attempt to delude it by referring to scholarship; and honest judges should not believe that their use of scholarship will hinder in any way their attempts to minimize their exercise of discretion. Used as it normally is (in hard cases or to reinforce arguments based on relatively clear mandatory sources), and selected in ways that do not require substantive deliberation (by looking to features like name of author, publishing company, etc.),

F. P. Shecaira, *Legal Scholarship as a Source of Law,*
SpringerBriefs in Law, DOI: 10.1007/978-3-319-00428-0_6,
© The Author(s) 2013

standard legal scholarship does not increase the amount of judicial discretion—in fact, it may even diminish it.

So, we should not construe the debate about when and how judges should be using legal scholarship as one about whether and to what extent judges should be exercising discretion. The typical arguments in favor of the view that judges should abide (whenever possible) by rules of positive law—e.g. arguments appealing to rule of law values such as predictability, non-arbitrariness, and fairness or formal justice (treating like cases alike)—cannot be used in favor of the view that judges should refrain from using legal scholarship. Also, to address the other side of the debate, defenders of judicial activism should not think that by enjoining judges to use scholarship they will be providing them with an effective means for defying formal rules of law that would otherwise constrain their decisions—unless, of course, advocates of activism propose a profound transformation in current conventions regarding the use of scholarship, by defending the use of non-standard, especially critical legal scholarship, even in easy cases and against the prescriptions flowing directly from mandatory sources.

On what, then, should scholars interested in normative questions about the use of legal scholarship be focusing? They should be focusing on things such as the general quality of the scholarship produced in the jurisdiction in question, the judges' capacity (given time constraints and limited resources) to engage carefully with the scholarship available to them,[1] the suitability of the (generally abstract and idealistic) academic approach to the practical questions with which different judges have to deal, and the legitimacy of allowing scholars (i.e. politically unaccountable actors tending to originate from social elites) to have a significant influence on the outcome of legal cases.

Needless to say, proper treatment of each of these issues, with the exception perhaps of the question of political legitimacy, requires great sensitivity to empirical inter- as well as intra-jurisdictional differences. The quality and usefulness of scholarship and the availability of the resources that judges need to adequately engage with it vary significantly across jurisdictions and even within jurisdictions: e.g. criminal law scholarship may be well developed in a country that does not have a comparable tradition in constitutional law scholarship; thus, judges in that country would likely be wise to treat their constitutional law scholars with less deference than their criminal law scholars. The topic of political legitimacy seems peculiar in that it admits of somewhat more general treatment. Societies whose broad political structures are similar will likely (and rightly) be sensitive to the same sorts of considerations. For instance, stable democracies with relatively

---

[1] For instance, the Brazilian Supreme Tribunal (recall their use of Claus Roxin) has often referred to German scholars of criminal law. But the court has been criticized by academic lawyers for misunderstanding the complex German scholarship to which it refers. It would pay to investigate what is generating misunderstanding and, on that basis, make recommendations as to how the court should deal with the relevant scholarship in the future. Shecaira (2013) has suggested that the court has displayed little sense of the historical context and purpose behind the theories of criminal law that it uses.

independent judiciaries will face the same sorts of concerns regarding the influence of scholars: especially in hard cases, one may wonder whether judges ought to be allowed to look for guidance in the opinions of non-state actors whose outlook (in virtue of their peculiar training and privileged social background) may not be representative of the views of the bulk of the population. Of course, things may be quite different in less democratic regimes; for in those regimes, the foregoing concern may be offset by an urgent need for progressive perspectives that only free-thinking intellectuals may be apt to provide.

It is important to note that there is little reason to believe that judges cannot figure out by themselves the appropriate answers at least to the more context-sensitive questions (the question of political legitimacy is arguably a tougher one which may divide sophisticated legal and political philosophers). Indeed, it appears that judges need no encouragement to seek scholarly influence in those jurisdictions characterized by circumstances making the use of scholarship seem more promising. Where lack of resources is not a problem and legal academic culture is vibrant, judges tend to help themselves to academic writings. And they also seem perfectly capable of identifying the best, most reliable sources among the numerous alternatives. Merryman (1977, 405–407), in a study of the citation practices of the California Supreme Court between 1950 and 1970, reports a significant rise in citation of law reviews and a comparable loss of popularity of traditional sources like the Restatement and encyclopedias. There are several possible reasons behind this trend. One of those reasons may be that the court acquired a greater freedom in managing its own docket and consequently developed a preference for those cases of "great social importance and those at the growing edge of the law", (ibid., 407) that is, precisely "the sort of law the legal periodicals rejoice in" (Ibid. 407). But another, equally plausible reason may simply be that the court grew suspicious of the often anonymously authored and non-peer-reviewed contributions to the Restatement and encyclopedias. Law reviews, especially the prominent ones preferred by American courts, seem indeed to contain works produced by the most diligent scholars with the best credentials. The members of the Supreme Court of California appear to have a sharp enough sense of what constitutes reliable scholarship; they do not need urgently to be lectured on the topic.[2]

---

[2] To be clear, my contention is simply that judges seem to have a pretty good handle on things. To say that judges need not be lectured is not to say that they have nothing to learn from scholars. Indeed, there has been a considerable amount of intricate argument among scholars about the standards to be employed in the evaluation of legal scholarship. Some of this argument occurs between those who defend formalist scholarship and those who oppose it in favor of purely normative, non-formalist writings (see, e.g., Alexander 1993). It is unlikely that many judges, given their typical allegiances, will be persuaded by those on the non-formalist side of this debate. But there are other kinds of arguments—for instance, that concerning the degree of methodological rigor to be sought by legal scholars whose work hinges on empirical theses (see, e.g., Goldsmith and Vermeule 2002)—which judges cannot ignore with impunity. These questions are important and complicated, and judges certainly have a lot to learn, as we all do, by heeding the work that has been produced recently in the field.

The only fairly specific recommendation I am willing to provide with respect to how scholarship ought to be used has to do with judicial honesty or transparency. In democratic societies, where the judiciary enjoys political independence relative to the other branches of government, and where judges do not typically struggle with the application of morally objectionable laws, there seems to exist a significant presumption in favor of judicial honesty. By making the true grounds of their decisions public judges show respect for the rational capacities of legal subjects. More precisely, they show respect for the "fundamental interest that citizens have in being governed according to reasons and principles to which they can give their considered assent" (Schwartzman 2008, 1004). Moreover, the practice of honest reason-giving seems conducive to a culture of open legal debate that is likely to have the effect of enhancing the general quality of judicial decision-making (ibid., 1010–1011, 1015).

Now, the presumption in favor of judicial honesty is not absolute and thus may occasionally be defeated. For judges should not disown the responsibility of pursuing important pragmatic goals such as the following:

> … to maintain the perceived legitimacy of the judiciary; to obtain public compliance with controversial judgments; to secure preferred outcomes through strategic action on multi-member courts; to promote the clarity, coherence, and continuity of legal doctrine; to avoid the destructive consequences of openly recognizing "tragic choices" between conflicting moral values; to preserve collegiality and civility in the courts; and to prevent the unnecessary proliferation of separate opinions (ibid., 988–989, footnotes omitted).

Indeed, if the perceived legitimacy or the very integrity of the courts is under a real threat, judges may be justified in being less than entirely transparent (although utter lying may be harder to argue for). One way that judges may mislead their audience is by suggesting that they are not exercising discretion (or at least not a great deal of it) when in fact they are. This is a purpose for which scholarship can fairly easily be co-opted. To be sure, the only reason why it can be so co-opted is that it in fact has the ability to reduce discretion when properly employed; for otherwise scholarship (like substantive arguments presented in formalist fashion) would be unlikely ever to serve as an effective smokescreen to hide the exercise of discretion.[3]

Unless there is a real threat of institutional crisis, and unless the only way to avert that threat involves the deceptive use of scholarship, judges ought not to use scholarship deceptively. How exactly might scholarship be used to deceive? One way is for a judge to defend a contentious formal or substantive argument by citing an author whose position is contested by other authors (unnamed in that judge's decision) of equally reputable status. Recall, for instance, the reference made by Wilson J. in *R v Morgentaler* to Sumner's view that the fetus should be viewed "in differential and developmental terms" ([1993] 3 S.C.R. 463, para 257), which was

---

[3] Notice the tension between the view I am proposing here and the account of legal scholarship suggested by the likes of Duxbury, Kötz, and Waddams. While those authors associate use of scholarship with activism, I am arguing that scholarship can be used in order to disguise activism.

followed by the indication that Sumner is a professor at the University of Toronto. Wilson's reference to Sumner has the potential to mislead. It should not be too hard to produce the opinion of a professor from a different and equally reputable university who disagrees with Professor Sumner. The issue is highly contentious but Wilson seems to suggest otherwise by providing a terse argument (if not the mere assertion of her own conclusion) followed by a single and unspecific reference to Sumner.

One might think of a possible reply to my criticism of Wilson's opinion. It could be argued that the Supreme Court of Canada maintains some convention restricting references by its members to the opinions of a limited class of scholars—for instance, moral and legal philosophers affiliated with the University of Toronto or equally respected Canadian universities. For in that case Wilson's use of Sumner's work could have been motivated by something other than her private sympathy for Summer's moral outlook. As far as I know, however, Wilson's court adheres to no such convention. And even if it did, Wilson would probably not be off the hook. Abortion is so controversial among moral and legal thinkers that there should be enough dissent within the University of Toronto itself for Wilson's terse reference to Sumner to remain misleading.

Consider another interesting Canadian example. In *R v Khela* the justices of the Supreme Court of Canada disagreed about how far trial judges should go in guiding juries about how to assess the evidence provided by the testimony of unreliable witnesses in criminal cases. The majority opinion argued that although "a jury's ability to evaluate the credibility of witnesses need not be 'micromanaged' by complex, mandated instructions" ([2009] 1 S.C.R. 104, para 28), juries should nevertheless be given a general framework within which to work. The majority timidly acknowledged that the relevant Supreme Court precedents did not conclusively favor their preferred framework, and, at a crucial step in their argument, affirmed the following (ibid., para 45–46):

> No benefit comes from a return to the overly rigid [instructions of the] pre-*Vetrovec* era. That said, the absence or presence of confirmatory evidence plays a key role in determining whether it is safe to rely on the testimony of an impugned witness (Harris, at p. 222). Accordingly, the instruction to the jury must make clear the type of evidence capable of offering support. It is not sufficient to simply tell the jury to look for whatever it feels confirms the truth of a witness' testimony (see *R. v. Chenier* (2006), 205 C.C.C. (3d) 333 (Ont. C.A.), at para 34).

Note that a paper by Nikos Harris, a criminal law scholar, and a decision by a provincial appellate court are the only sources to which the majority directly referred in order to establish the argument that *some* instruction (i.e. the kind that can be offered by their proposed framework), but not overly rigid instructions, is to be given to juries by trial judges. In her partially concurring reasons, Deschamps J. worried that by establishing even that *some* instruction be provided, the majority was threatening the highly desirable flexibility and simplicity of the rules of evidence bearing on the assessment of testimony of unreliable witnesses. In contrast to the majority, Deschamps was very emphatic about the equivocal nature of case law on the matter, and she pointed out that commentators had also disagreed about how to interpret the relevant precedents. Indeed, Deschamps made reference to three other authors in addition to Harris (the sole author cited by the majority).

The lesson to be extracted from this account of *R v Khela* is the following. In the absence of Deschamps's argument, the reader of the majority opinion might have come away with the impression that the case hinged on a point of law that was not perfectly settled by binding precedent but which benefited from the decision of a lower court and the opinion of an expert. Deschamps came to the rescue of the uninformed reader by emphasizing the indeterminacy of case law and the related lack of consensus among experts. *R v Khela*, in so far as the majority opinion is concerned, is a good example of how scholarship can be used in a misleading way. We need Deschamps's opinion in order to appreciate the true extent of the majority's exercise of discretion (To her credit, Deschamps quite candidly provided a clearly substantive argument in her defense of the preservation of the simplicity of evidence law: "The justice system should strive for simplicity. In long trials, which have become common where serious charges are laid, every added level of complexity increases the risk of error for both the trial judge and the jury" (ibid., para 91). To be clear, I am not praising Deschamps merely for resorting to substantive argument. I am praising her for not trying to hide the fact that she was doing so in a case where, given the indeterminacy of the applicable positive law, she could hardly avoid it).

In conclusion, it may be instructive to contrast the aforementioned misuses of legal scholarship with an example of a judicial decision in which scholarship is used in a responsible and transparent manner. In the case already mentioned of *R v Kapp*, a question arose as to the correct interpretation of section 15(2) of the Canadian Charter of Rights and Freedoms. The majority wanted to argue that where the Charter speaks of a law or program's having as its "object the amelioration of conditions of disadvantaged individuals or groups", it speaks of the law or program's purpose, not of its actual effects. For the majority, the constitutionality of an affirmative action program is to be assessed on the basis of the merits of its (credible) aims, not on whether it is successful in realizing those aims. The majority began by acknowledging the existence of scholarly disagreement on the matter ([2008] 2 S.C.R. 483, para 44–45), and then engaged a substantive argument proposed by those scholars who associate the "object" of affirmative action programs with their actual effects. In articulating the steps of its counter-argument, the majority found support in sympathetic decisions issued by lower courts.

The point is that the majority in *R v Kapp* had the ability to refer exclusively to those scholars that favored their own interpretation of section 15(2). But, unlike the majority in *R v Khela*, it acknowledged the existence of scholarly dissent, and openly pursued the substantive issue (relying, to the extent that it could, on non-binding precedent). It is important to note that, had there been scholarly consensus on the matter, the majority in *R v Kapp* would likely have acted differently. For elsewhere in that same decision the majority appeared to be quite deferential to the dominant scholarly opinion (recall my discussion of *R v Kapp* in Chap. 4); but fortunately it seemed to realize that it could only (candidly) defer to scholars when they did not disagree among themselves.

References

Alexander L (1993) What we do, and why we do it. Stanford Law Rev 45:1885

Goldsmith J, Vermeule A (2002) Empirical methodology and legal scholarship. Univ Chicago Law Rev 69:153

Merryman JH (1977) Toward a theory of citations: an empirical study of the citation practice of the California Supreme Court in 1950, 1960, and 1970. South Calif Law Rev 50:381

Schwartzman M (2008) Judicial sincerity. Va Law Rev 94:987

Shecaira S (2013) Nihil humani a me alienum puto. Boletim IBCCRIM No 243, Fevereiro/2013. Available at http://www.ibccrim.org.br/site/boletim/capa.php?bol_id=284. Accessed on 01 February 2013

Chapter 7
Conclusion

In a nutshell, sources of law are sources of norms systematically treated by judges as content-independent reasons for action. Those reasons need not be authoritative in order for their sources to be sources *of law*; for a source to deserve that qualification it need only produce content-independent reasons for action. Although authoritativeness is not an essential feature of the reasons produced by sources of law, the distinction between authoritative and non-authoritative content-independent reasons is crucial for understanding the important distinction between mandatory and permissive sources of law—which may also be rendered as a threefold distinction between "must-", "should-", and "may-sources". Another important feature of my account of sources of law is the insight that the "must" and the "may" in the foregoing phrases refer to the use of the relevant sources and not to the enforcement of the norms which they generate; the latter should be associated with "shoulds"—a strong, authoritative "should" in the case of mandatory sources and a weaker one in the case of permissive sources.

The main ambition of this study, in addition to providing a general account of what sources of law are and how they are to be identified, was to argue that (standard) legal scholarship sometimes functions as a source of law in different jurisdictions. This is an empirical thesis about the use of legal scholarship by courts of law whose defense depended on a fair amount of preliminary conceptual work. Indeed, to give an example of such conceptual work, legal theorists have been distracted by differences between scholarship and other undisputed instances of sources of law (such as legislation, judicial precedent, and custom) that, although not negligible, serve to obscure the crucial similarity that exists between them. Scholarship can guide judicial decision-making by producing content-independent reasons (just like legislation and precedent and custom can) even if (unlike legislation and precedent and custom) scholarship itself is not produced by accountable agents of the state and its influence is ultimately grounded on its persuasiveness. Thus, scholarship is undeniably a peculiar source of law, but it shares with the standard instances of sources of law that which is the essential feature of all such instances. Merryman (to quote him again) put the point quite aptly: "It is possible for cases to be decided, rules of law to be stated, lines of

F. P. Shecaira, *Legal Scholarship as a Source of Law*,
SpringerBriefs in Law, DOI: 10.1007/978-3-319-00428-0_7,
© The Author(s) 2013

decision begun and perpetuated, solely on the authority of a textual treatment having its origins [in legal scholarship]".

This book contains at least two more noteworthy claims pertaining to the use of legal scholarship by judges. First, it challenges the idea that self-effacing judges are likely to avoid using legal scholarship in the justification of their decisions. This challenge is important in its own right, insofar as it opposes a notion that appears to be taken for granted by influential comparative lawyers; and it is also important as part of an attempt to understand more fully the notion of legal scholarship as a source of law—in particular, it allows us to see that legal scholarship can be used to *limit* the exercise of discretion by judges. The second and related claim defended in this study is that judges who are aware of scholarship's discretion-curbing potential can (and sometimes do) deceptively invoke it to suggest that they are not exercising discretion (or much discretion) when in fact they are. "Deception" is normally used as an evaluative term, and it is not stripped of its evaluative significance here. By describing some uses of scholarship as deceptive I suggest that they ought morally to be avoided at least in democratic societies where judges are subject to a strong presumption in favor of argumentative candor.

A number of objections can be made against my account of legal scholarship as a source of law. Some of these objections were addressed (and hopefully refuted) in the course of the book. There are other objections, however, which have been left to the end. Although distinct, I believe these objections are based on the same fundamental error: they mistake puzzles about the more general notion of a source of law for puzzles that apply particularly to the notion of legal scholarship as a source of law. Some of these puzzles are more easily resolved, and therefore (once I have shown how they are resolved) need not worry us at all. Others may be more difficult, but the fact that they are not peculiar to legal scholarship as a source of law is still very important. For if these more difficult puzzles were taken to be damning (which probably they should not be), then they would require that one abandon the very notion of a source of law or at least that some standard instances of sources of law be disqualified as such—and these are not trivial moves given the prominence that the notion of a source of law has long enjoyed in legal theory. So, even if the more general notion of a source of law were fraught with irresolvable problems (which it likely is not), my own project in this work would remain somewhat sheltered from criticism; for an otherwise unimpressive attack against my modest account of legal scholarship as a source of law would, if based on the relevant objections, imply an intrepid assault on the established general notion of a source of law.

Let me begin with an example of an objection resting on a relatively easily resolved puzzle. It has been suggested to me on different occasions that legal scholarship's function is to produce knowledge about what the law *is*. Scholars, the argument goes, are here to discover and report those of law's requirements which are not easily discerned by non-experts. To the extent that scholars have any authority, they have only theoretical authority; they simply know more than the ordinary person, and even the ordinary legal professional, about how to decipher the law when it is cryptic. There are authors who have put such a view in print in terms that are nearly as explicit. Regla (2000), for instance, conceives of jurists as expert applicants of the "legal method", i.e. a method of argument—but not of norm-creation—used to derive "implicit" law from "explicit" law.

Before I reply to the objection at hand, there is an important issue that needs to be clarified. The view being contrasted with my position asserts that legal scholars are theoretical authorities since they only generate reasons for belief about the law's current content. This view is to be distinguished from a different view which is not incompatible with my position, namely, that scholars may give reasons for belief about how cases ought to be decided. I have argued that scholars may be sources of (content-independent) reasons *for action*. Reasons for belief about what ought to be done are admittedly not identical with reasons for action: indeed one may be justified in one's practical beliefs and yet fail to be justified in how one acts (i.e. one may conceivably fail to act well in spite of not making any epistemic mistake in the course of assessing the correctness of one's action). But remember that my inquiry is not normative: it is not about what reasons (theoretical or practical) judges actually have, but rather about what reasons they take themselves to have. Presumably, a judge who takes himself to have reason to believe that he ought to act a certain way also takes himself to have reason to act in that way. This is not a conceptual claim to the effect that one thing entails the other; it is an empirical claim to the effect that the two typically come together. The subtle difference that exists between reasons for holding practical beliefs and reasons for action is of little importance within the context of an intellectual enterprise whose principal purpose is to discuss how it is that judges use certain sources of law.

Let us come back to the objection now. There is no argument, indeed, that scholars sometimes do no more than report existing legal norms. But my view is that this is not all they do. Indeed, it is my impression that this is not even what they most often do (i.e. this is not what *standard* legal scholarship is about). When a scholar interprets a vague or ambiguous statute or unifies several precedents under a potentially controversial general principle, he often does more than simply report what other authorities have established. Indeed, he contributes to the creation of something new; and if judges systematically heed that scholar's contributions and let themselves be guided by them (in the belief that they ought to let themselves be guided by them), then that scholar will effectively be contributing to the creation of *new law*.

How does the objection at issue suffer from the flaw of mistaking a more general problem about sources of law for a problem about legal scholarship as a source of law? Well, the objection implies a type of formalism about legal scholarship that is grounded on the same sort of outlook that prompts the now infamous formalism concerning judicial decision-making. I use "formalism" here in the pejorative sense of dubious denial of choice. Legal scholars, as I argued in Chap. 4, act much like judges do. They do not argue as freely as political theorists (say) but let their reasoning be hedged by rules deriving from conventional sources of law. Now, even when judicial and scholarly reference to such rules is sincere (that is, when they are not simply trying to disguise their purely moral or political reasoning under a glossy varnish of legalism), judges and scholars are not entirely prevented from making choices, i.e. from filling in gaps or reshaping and developing existing law by appeal to controversial substantive considerations. This is something which should be uncontroversial when it comes to judicial decisions. Judges do decide on the basis of statute and precedent, but they also fill in the pores of such sources, as well as rebuild and develop their non-porous parts. Their ability to do this is admittedly circumscribed, but it still exists. That is why today we speak confidently of the existence of case law; that is why we take judicial decisions to be sources of law, even if they are not made in a vacuum but within a relatively rigid framework of rules. Scholars, to repeat, argue much like judges. They work within a normative framework whose rigidity is significant but does not entirely prevent the exercise of choice. To be a formalist about legal scholarship is perhaps not yet outdated; but it is as wrongheaded (and for precisely the same reasons) as subscribing to the outdated type of formalism that concerns judicial decision-making.[1]

Now, this may seem to imply that scholarship can only function as a source of law when it serves either a gap-filling or a reforming purpose. But was it not suggested, in Chap. 4, that scholarship can also function as a source of law when it is used to reinforce, or give additional support to, decisions which are fairly well supported by standard sources like statutes and precedents? Indeed, I maintain that scholarship can also function as a source of law when it is not filling in the gaps of or reforming existing law, as long as it is not being used merely to report the content of the statutes and precedents that alone ground the decision. One has to be attentive to whether a judge is citing a scholarly writing because, say, there is no usable official report of a relevant precedent,[2] or rather because he thinks the scholar's opinion renders the precedent's prescription even more compelling. Anyone who finds it suspicious that the same decision could be grounded on, say, precedent *and* scholarship is, again, voicing a doubt that does not refer exclusively to scholarship's capacity to function as a source of law. This is in fact a more general doubt about whether *any two* sources of law retain their independence once cumulated in a judicial opinion. What happens when a judge grounds a decision on statute *and* precedent (on the assumption that he does not take "precedent" as a mere report of the norm explicit in the statute)? Should we doubt that he is using *two* sources of law instead of one? Whether the answer is "yes" or "no" (my own intuition is "no"), the point is that the problem is not peculiar to legal scholarship and the special ways in which it is used by judges.

Consider now an objection based on a more difficult puzzle. One might argue that, in modern legal systems, the secondary rules specifying standard sources of law like statutes and judicial precedents are surrounded by fairly precise ancillary

---

[1] For a sophisticated critique of formalism with respect to legal scholarship, see Nino (1974, Chaps. 3 and 4), focusing on criminal law scholarship in a civil law culture.

[2] This may happen, for instance, when a judge relies on a foreign judicial decision translated by a comparative lawyer. The translator may add nothing to the foreign court's argument; his only contribution is to make the decision accessible.

secondary rules governing law-making procedure and guiding those who want to study the relevant products in an attempt to find the norms they establish. In modern legal systems we know not only that legislation is a source of law, but we know quite precisely how legislation is produced, in what forms it appears, what bits of it are to be heeded by courts of law, and so on. When it comes to legal scholarship, however, things are much more lax. So, we might know that Pollock is an authority. But which of his writings are to be heeded? And what parts of his writings? Are we to read entire books or essays by Pollock (in contrast to seeking specific provisions in a piece of legislation) in search of the opinions which might give rise to legally relevant norms? When Pollock writes something that has the potential to serve as a source of law, how are we to know? Is the event somehow made public in anything like the way that the enactment of legislation and the issuance of judicial decisions are made public? The upshot of the objection is that, in the absence of ancillary rules guiding one in the use of scholarly writings, scholarship is a conceivable source of law which is actually too unwieldy to serve the practical needs of legal professionals.

My response to this objection is not to deny that it can be hard to use legal scholarship as a source of law, but to point out that the contrast between scholarship and standard sources is exaggerated. There simply is not in modern legal systems such an abundance of precise secondary rules guiding legal professionals in their attempt to extract norms from agreed-upon sources of law. Just consider how controversial the question is whether any complex legal system contains precise rules about the interpretation of statutes. I have indicated my own belief that most legal systems contain an interpretive rule establishing a presumption in favor of plain meaning, a presumption that can be defeated if the enforcement of plain meaning leads to substantively very unsatisfactory results or is in tension with clear legislative intention or agreed-upon statutory purpose. But notice how vague this rule is; and notice also that many authors would likely think I am being too optimistic in believing that most legal systems contain any interpretive rule as precise as this one: as vague as the rule is, it may be argued that I am actually underestimating its vagueness. It may also be argued that I am mistaking for a *rule* what really is no more than a "maxim of practical interpretative wisdom" which "does not provide any simple binary directive about right and wrong interpretations in difficult cases" (MacCormick 1993, 27). Matters are even more complicated with respect to judicial precedent. Just think of the never-ending debates about how one is to determine the *ratio decidendi* or the holding of a case, that is to say, the bits of a written judicial decision that (in contrast with *obiter dicta*) are binding for other courts of law or for the same court in the future.

So, there is also an important lack of secondary rules governing the use of standard sources of law. And yet few people would deny that legislation and precedent are clear instances of sources of law. Perhaps the reason for this is that, in spite of perennial difficulties in formulating general interpretive and related secondary rules, there is often (and I would dare say, most of the time) little disagreement or doubt about what norms are effectively established by statutes and precedents. We may have trouble formulating the rationale behind our interpretive activities, but we have the relevant know-how.

These are just a few examples of objections resting on the mistake of assigning to an account of a peculiar, non-standard source of law the (more or less difficult) problems that affect the very notion of a source of law or, more precisely in respect of the particular examples given here, problems that could put in doubt the classification as a source of law of even the paradigm instances of this concept. Other examples could be given, as I have been confronted with other objections resting on the same mistake in conversations with different colleagues. They are not mentioned here because they seem less interesting and fruitful than the examples given above (One interesting objection not discussed here was dealt with indirectly in Chap. 3. It consists in the claim that legal scholarship cannot produce content-independent reasons because scholars do not write with the specific intention that their views be regarded by judges as content-independent reasons. This objection clearly ignores the possibility that prescriptions may be content-independent-reason-giving in reception albeit not in creation. Relatedly, it implies paradoxically that custom, a standard example of a source of (unintentionally created) law is really no source of law at all).

I conclude, thus, with the plea that before the skeptical reader reaches a verdict on the merits of the account of scholarship as a source of law advanced in this book, he consider whether any of its potential flaws are unique to it or instead whether they are applicable to any general account of sources of law—indeed, to the very account which the reader likely endorses as a central part of his or her jurisprudence.

References

MacCormick N (1993) Argumentation and interpretation in law. Ratio Juris 6:16

Nino CS (1974) Consideraciones sobre la Dogmática Jurídica. UNAM, México

Regla JA (2000) Teoría General de las Fuentes del Derecho (y del Orden Jurídico). Ariel, Barcelona